"Who Do Men Say That I Am?"

"Who Do Men Say That I Am?"

A Study of Jesus

By
Susanna Wilder Heinz

Beacon Press   Boston

Author's Foreword

How much can we really know about Jesus? How can we tell whether what we read in the many books about his life and teachings is true? Which of the many portrayals of Jesus should we accept? How can we choose?

It is to help answer these questions, and others like them, that this book was written. It is designed primarily for use in a group. The comparison of answers and the testing of one's opinion against that of someone else is valuable in a search such at this. It is not essential, however. The individual reader may derive pleasure and benefit from answering for himself the questions posed.

This is a book to be enjoyed. It is to be taken seriously, but not solemnly, for the pursuit of truth is a joyous experience, difficult at times but always fascinating. In this pursuit the reader must be a detective, shifting the evidence with a critical eye. It is important, therefore, that all the questions which are asked in the book be answered. Those who skip the "hard" ones will be leaving out a piece which may be important in the final picture. Some of the "easy" ones are included so that an obvious piece of information may not be overlooked. If after finishing it, the reader has found some of the problems in the way of his understanding and appreciation of Jesus solved, and a portrait of him emerging which is the reader's own, this book will have served its purpose.

The Revised Standard Version of the New Testament has been used in this book, but another translation of the Bible can be substituted. It is, in fact, often helpful to compare translations since this in some measure makes up for the fact that we are not reading in the original Greek.

The order of the quotations from the Synoptics is chronological rather than in the order they appear in the New Testament. Therefore, Mark is first, then Matthew, and then Luke.

Most of the people who have contributed to this book must remain anonymous. They include those childhood playmates of mine who had strong opinions on what one should believe about Jesus, and whose expressions of shock that I did not share them caused me to wonder what the truth about him was. I was all the more curious because their opinions were not shared with each other, but differed. Which one was right? Or was I?

Many teachers have added to my knowledge of the New Testament and of Jesus. There were my Sunday School teachers, and the ministers whose sermons I heard. There were my college professors and my graduate school professors who shared their knowledge with me, and more important, helped me form my own opinions based on my own research and study. There were also the authors of the many books I have read whose influence cannot be identified for it has become so much a part of my thinking. There were also my former students, and the children in the Church Schools which I have been privileged to direct, who have tested my ability to explain to others what I have learned, and in the process have taught me even more.

There are still others for whose specific help with this book I give my thanks, although none of them is in any way responsible for the final results: Dorothy T. Spoerl, Curriculum Editor of the Division of Education, Unitarian Universalist Association, without whose constant encouragement and energetic work this book would have been impossible; Charles C. Forman, Minister of the First Parish in Plymouth, whose knowledgeable criticism made this a far more interesting study than it would have been otherwise; Sophia Lyon

Fahs, whose insight and wisdom helped greatly in the initial stages of this work; Webster L. Kitchell, Minister of the Eliot Chapel, Kirkwood, Missouri, whose reading of the manuscript and comments on it were most helpful; and Florence McKinlay, whose careful and meticulous reading of the manuscript improved it immensely.

I would also like to thank the following Unitarian Church Schools where parts of the manuscript were tried out, and whose comment, criticisms and suggestions have been appreciated: Oklahoma City, Oklahoma; Rochester, New York; Dallas, Texas; White Plains, New York; Stamford, Connecticut; and Unitarian Church of All Souls, New York City.

Finally to my husband Bernard, who read the first draft and helped to clarify many of the ideas expressed and who has endured so patiently the vicissitudes of having an author-wife, my love and appreciation.

S. W. H.

Port Washington, New York

Contents

List of Illustrations

"Who Do Men Say That I Am?"

"And Jesus went on with his disciples to the villages of Caesarea Philippi; and on the way he asked his disciples, "Who do men say that I am?" And they told him, "John the Baptist; and others say, Elijah; and others one of the prophets." And he asked them, "But who do you say that I am?"

Mark 8:27-29
Revised Standard Version

Chapter One:

Have You Ever Wondered?

Have you ever wondered as you sang Christmas carols how the events which we sing about at Christmas happened, and why they are important? Perhaps you have always taken for granted the celebration of Christmas with its carols, pageants and joyful church services, and never wondered about them. Or it may be that in your life the celebration of this holiday centered around your home and Santa Claus, mistletoe, Christmas trees and presents.

You could not live in today's world and have any friends, however, without being aware that Christmas is an important religious holiday, as well as an ancient festival connected with the winter solstice. Christian churches commemorate the birth of Jesus and celebrate Christmas according to their various traditions. How much do we *really* know about the birthday of Jesus: the date, the place and the events which are reported as having occurred at the time?

Here are some questions to which we might seek the answers:

Who were Jesus' parents?
Did he have any brothers or sisters?
Where was he born?
When?
Where are we told about the shepherds and the kings coming to see the baby Jesus?

3

What is the "flight into Egypt"? The "slaughter of the innocents"?

Try to answer these questions before you go any further. Write down your answers and keep them to refer to later. Add and answer any other questions you may have about the birth of Jesus.

How are we going to find the answers to these questions? If we are to learn facts about the birth of Jesus, it is logical that we should go to the only sources which tell us about the life of Jesus. These sources are, of course, the four Gospels found in the beginning of the New Testament. Let us look at them to see what they have to tell us.

The Genealogies

Turn to the New Testament and examine the first part of each of the four Gospels. With what event in the life of Jesus does each begin? Judging from the openings, how many of the Gospels do you think will be useful in answering our questions?

Let's begin by asking who Jesus' parents were. When a person wants to learn about his ancestry, he usually looks up his genealogy or family tree. Perhaps we are in luck in learning about Jesus, because there are two genealogies for him, one in Matthew and one in Luke. The chart which follows shows the family lines clearly. Study it and compare it with the Bible record in Matthew 1 and in Luke 3: 23-38.

How do the two records compare?
Do you think they are reliable?
Can you think of any reason why Matthew would trace the ancestry of Jesus to Abraham while Luke traces his descent from Adam?

The Genealogies

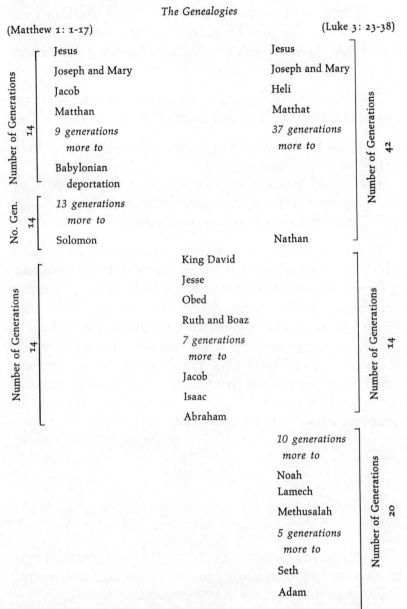

(Matthew 1: 1-17)

(Luke 3: 23-38)

Number of Generations — 14

Jesus

Joseph and Mary

Jacob

Matthan

9 generations more to

Babylonian deportation

No. Gen. — 14

13 generations more to

Solomon

Number of Generations — 14

King David

Jesse

Obed

Ruth and Boaz

7 generations more to

Jacob

Isaac

Abraham

Number of Generations — 42

Jesus

Joseph and Mary

Heli

Matthat

37 generations more to

Nathan

Number of Generations — 14

Number of Generations — 20

10 generations more to

Noah

Lamech

Methusalah

5 generations more to

Seth

Adam

Note:

1. The Matthew Genealogy has been reversed to make comparison easier.

2. To make the section with the name of Jesus in it come out 14 generations as Matthew states it should, Mary has to be counted as a separate generation or Christ must be.

5

Is there any reason why both genealogies would include David, the great king, among Jesus' ancestors?

What do you think the "as was supposed" means in Luke 3:23?

To answer this last question, we need to compare two passages: Matthew 1: 18-25 and Luke 1: 26-34.

If you read only these passages who would you think was the father of Jesus?

Why do you suppose these writers were anxious to show that Jesus was miraculously born?

Did Jesus have any brothers and sisters?

To answer this last question, you could use a concordance which is a book which lists the words used in the Bible and gives the references so that you can look them up. In case you do not have a concordance, here are some passages which you can read to answer the question. If you do have a concordance, check and see if any references have been omitted. Mark 6:3 and Mark 3:31-35 (if you are using a Revised Standard Version of the New Testament, be sure to read the footnote). Check also: Matthew 12:46-50 and 13:53-57. In Luke read 8:19-21 and in Acts 1:14.

The Birth of Jesus

The questions concerning the actual birth of Jesus can best be answered by comparing the two versions of that event. They are printed here for your convenience.

Matthew 2

1 Now when Jesus was born in Bethlehem of Judea in the days of Herod the king, behold, wise men from the East came to Jerusalem,

El Greco (Spanish, 1541 – 1614), The Adoration of the Shepherds
The Metropolitan Museum of Art, bequest of George Blumenthal, 1941

7

saying,[2] "Where is he who has been born king of the Jews? For we have seen his star in the East, and have come to worship him."[3] When Herod the king heard this, he was troubled, and all Jerusalem with him;[4] and assembling all the chief priests and scribes of the people, he inquired of them where the Christ was to be born.[5] They told him, "In Bethlehem of Judea; for so it is written by the prophet:

[6]'And you, O Bethlehem, in the land of Judah,
are by no means least among the rulers of Judah;
for from you shall come a ruler
who will govern my people Israel.' "

7 Then Herod summoned the wise men secretly and ascertained from them what time the star appeared;[8] and he sent them to Bethlehem, saying, "Go and search diligently for the child, and when you have found him bring me word, that I too may come and worship him." [9] When they had heard the king they went their way; and lo, the star which they had seen in the East went before them, till it came to rest over the place where the child was.[10] When they saw the star, they rejoiced exceedingly with great joy;[11] and going into the house they saw the child with Mary his mother, and they fell down and worshiped him. Then, opening their treasures, they offered him gifts, gold and frankincense and myrrh.[12] And being warned in a dream not to return to Herod, they departed to their own country by another way.

13 Now when they had departed, behold, an angel of the Lord appeared to Joseph in a dream and said, "Rise, take the child and his mother, and flee to Egypt, and remain there till I tell you; for Herod is about to search for the child, to destroy him." [14]And he rose and took the child and his mother by night, and departed to Egypt, [15]and remained there until the death of Herod. This was to fulfil what the Lord had spoken by the prophet, "Out of Egypt have I called my son."

16 Then Herod, when he saw that he had been tricked by the wise men, was in a furious rage, and he sent and killed all the male children in Bethlehem and in all that region who were two years old or under, according to the time which he had ascertained from the wise men. [17]Then was fulfilled what was spoken by the prophet Jeremiah:

[18]"A voice was heard in Ramah,
wailing and loud lamentation,
Rachel weeping for her children;
she refused to be consoled,
because they were no more."

19 But when Herod died, behold, an angel of the Lord appeared in a dream to Joseph in Egypt, saying, [20]"Rise, take the child and his mother, and go to the land of Israel, for those who sought the child's life

are dead." ²¹And he rose and took the child and his mother, and went to the land of Israel. ²² But when he heard that Archelaus reigned over Judea in place of his father Herod, he was afraid to go there, and being warned in a dream he withdrew to the district of Galilee. ²³And he went and dwelt in a city called Nazareth, that what was spoken by the prophets might be fulfilled, "He shall be called a Nazarene."

Luke 2: 1-20

1 In those days a decree went out from Caesar Augustus that all the world should be enrolled. ² This was the first enrollment, when Quirinius was governor of Syria. ³And all went to be enrolled, each to his own city. ⁴And Joseph also went up from Galilee, from the city of Nazareth, to Judea, to the city of David, which is called Bethlehem, because he was of the house and lineage of David, ⁵to be enrolled with Mary, his betrothed, who was with child. ⁶And while they were there, the time came for her to be delivered. ⁷And she gave birth to her first-born son and wrapped him in swaddling cloths, and laid him in a manger, because there was no place for them in the inn.

8 And in that region there were shepherds out in the field, keeping watch over their flock by night. ⁹And an angel of the Lord appeared to them and the glory of the Lord shone around them, and they were filled with fear. ¹⁰And the angel said to them, "Be not afraid; for behold, I bring you good news of a great joy which will come to all the people; ¹¹for to you is born this day in the city of David a Savior, who is Christ the Lord. ¹²And this will be a sign for you: you will find a babe wrapped in swaddling cloths and lying in a manger." ¹³And suddenly there was with the angel a multitude of the heavenly host praising God and saying,

¹⁴"Glory to God in the highest,
and on earth peace among men with whom he is pleased!"

15 When the angels went away from them into heaven, the shepherds said to one another, "Let us go over to Bethlehem and see this thing that has happened, which the Lord has made known to us." ¹⁶And they went with haste, and found Mary and Joseph, and the babe lying in a manger. ¹⁷And when they saw it they made known the saying which had been told them concerning this child; ¹⁸and all who heard it wondered at what the shepherds told them. ¹⁹But Mary kept all these things, pondering them in her heart. ²⁰And the shepherds returned, glorifying and praising God for all they had heard and seen, as it had been told them.

Where was Jesus born?

Why does Matthew say he was born there? Luke?
Who does Matthew say came to worship the baby?
How did they know about him?
Who does Luke say came? How did they know?
What is the "flight into Egypt"? The "slaughter of the innocents"?
When was Jesus born?
What do these passages tell which might be of help in establishing the date?
What information do we need which is not included?

Now that we have examined the records, we might pause before we go on and see what we *have* learned about the birth of Jesus. How many of the list of questions to which we were seeking answers have we answered? This is a good time to make another list of questions: Questions Raised by Our Attempting to Answer the First Questions! Take time to do this.

It is obvious that if we are to learn about Jesus, we need to have more information than we can find in the Gospels. There are puzzling contradictions in them. We need to know why this is so, and we need help in interpretation. There are references to men and events which the people for whom the Gospels were written apparently knew about, but which we do not. We need to know who these men were and when the events referred to happened in order to arrive at any dates. There are ideas reflected in these passages, too, which once understood will open the door to greater understanding of the passages themselves.

So let's set aside the notes we have made. We will come back to them at a later date to see if we can answer some of the questions we have had to leave unanswered for the moment.

Fra Angelico (Italian, Florentine, 1387 – 1455), The Nativity
The Metropolitan Museum of Art, Rogers Fund, 1924

Chapter Two:

Widely Differing Reports

We will have to journey back into time, to a small country on the easternmost shores of the Mediterranean Sea to find what traces we can of a life which was lived there, a life which was destined to change the world. We are seeking to learn about Jesus. He lived in the earliest part of the first century. He wrote no books. He had no contemporary biographer. The only records we have of his life were handed down by word of mouth for many years after his death. The Gospels, which give us the record of his life, were written, not with accuracy of detail in mind, but with the needs of the followers of the religion which he inspired as their concern. Yet, we can find here recorded some of the facts, some of the words which will help us distinguish the figure we seek.

This search will not be easy. Many have made it, and from them have come widely differing reports of what this man was like. It is probable that as we explore for ourselves the traces of Jesus' life, we, too, will ultimately arrive at widely differing interpretations of this man of Galilee.

There are many who have told us about Jesus. Their reasons for studying his life are as many as their findings about that life are varied. What do some of these people tell us about his nature?

"The Crucified Christ"

There are those who speak to us of the Crucified Christ. They quote the words of the author of the Gospel of John,

"God so loved the world that he gave his only Son, that whoever believes in him should not perish but have eternal life" (John 3:16). For these people a belief in the man of Galilee as the Son of God is the center of faith. According to them his life was the gift of God to sinful mankind in order to bring about a reconciliation between God and man which could only come through the grace of God, himself. They believe that Jesus laid down his life for us that through faith in him we might have eternal life in the world to come. What greater motivation than this belief could there be for the study of every detail of that earthly life? Evidence found in the Gospels of a miraculous birth has deep and abiding meaning for these people. They follow the footsteps of Jesus as he taught, and feel anew his awareness of his close relationship with God. They sorrow at the foot of the cross as he is crucified, a sacrifice for us all, and finally they rejoice in the resurrection which speaks of the triumph over death. For them, this is to come again into the presence of the greatest miracle ever known. For those of this faith, no further urging is needed to persuade them to turn again and again to the Gospel records to learn all they can of this unique life.

"The Perfect Life"

There are others who speak to us of Jesus of Nazareth. They are those whose study of the New Testament pages is a search for deeper understanding of a man whom they consider to be the greatest of all men. This greatness for them lies not in miracle, nor in his separateness from the main stream of mankind, but in the fact that here was a man who lived a life that influenced future generations, century upon century. To these seekers, the importance of the study of the life of Jesus lies in the importance of the search for the eternal values which he taught. For them to find more of the truth which he spoke and which he lived day by day in the short life which was granted to him, is to be helped to emulate the most perfect life ever lived.

"The Great Religious Teacher"

Others have told us of the Great Religious Teacher. In their search through the sacred writings of many religions, they have found the same ethical and spiritual truths repeated again and again. On occasion, however, a religious leader shares with his followers new insights which reveal another facet of truth. Such a man was Guatama Buddha, such a man Confucius, such a man Mohammed. So also was Jesus. Each gathered about him disciples who carried forward his teaching until, as succeeding generations followed one after another, the man himself became obscured in myth and legend. To uncover once more the truths which these men revealed, and to come close to them as human beings, is to add another stone to the ever enlarging, never to be finished, building of religious knowledge.

"The Prophet"

There are still others who talk to us of The Prophet. Some of them say that Jesus was the greatest prophet of them all, while others point to the long line of prophets in the Old Testament. Amos, Hosea, Isaiah, Jeremiah are in the great prophetic tradition. To some, Jesus stands in this tradition. When they look at the pages of the New Testament, they see again the same kind of impatience, with hypocrisy and superficiality and disdain of God's will, which is found in the pages of the Old Testament. Those who picture Jesus as a prophet hear one single prophetic voice which speaks to our time.

Many others speak to us of Jesus, each with his own reason for seeking knowledge about this man. Each has his own idea of the real importance of that life in Palestine and each has created his own picture of what this man was like.

One might feel that with all the conflicting images of him, it would be a hopeless task to attempt to reconstruct his life, yet we need to do this, for all around us is evidence of his influence. The dating of our years, the paintings in our art galleries, the music of our great composers, the customs we observe, the very history of our Western culture, all reflect in various ways that life. We cannot live in the Western world without feeling his influence. How shall we understand our own time and culture if we ourselves do not learn what we can about him?

The Artists' Interpretations

A tour through an art gallery, or the study of a collection of pictures of paintings and statues by the great masters, will reveal how much the artists rely upon the events of the life of Jesus as they are recorded in the New Testament. In the centuries since the crucifixion, how many paintings have been made of that event? These range from stark representations of the three crosses on the hill to elaborate *Pietàs* with the figure of Mary and the women clasping the dead body of Jesus to them, with all of the grief and agony traced on their faces in lifelike detail.

Nativity in a Gothic setting, from early sixteenth century Hours of the
   Virgin
Courtesy of the Pierpont Morgan Library

How many madonnas have been painted or sculptured? Fat ones, thin ones, Italian ones and Chinese ones—all attempts to depict the beauty of the Virgin Mary and the age-old mystery of life itself in the features of a little baby.

Or, perhaps, our eye is caught by some of the seemingly endless variety of nativity scenes. Some of these are sentimental, some are simple, some are elaborate; many of them make it seem that the nativity took place in the artist's own time and land. Many artists have chosen the myths which surround the nativity for their theme rather than the birth story itself: the flight into Egypt, the wise men following the star, the shepherds and the angel, and others which will not be found in the pages of the New Testament, but which have come down from the apocryphal stories.

Other artists have chosen Jesus preaching to the multitudes, Jesus walking on the water, Jesus healing the blind, Jesus with his disciples, the transfiguration, the entry into Jerusalem, or the resurrection. All of these events have been imagined countless times. The man of Galilee speaks to us still through the talents of our greatest artists.

Yet our study of the artists' interpretation of the life and spirit of Jesus need not be confined to the great masters. Many others have tried in their own ways to present to the eye something of their feeling and devotion for him. In statues and stained glass windows, in Sunday School cards and illustrated lives of Jesus, in posters urging us to go to church, and on Christmas cards we see his life illustrated—sometimes well, often not. If we have eyes to see, we must be aware of the ever present figure of Jesus.

The graphic artist is not alone among the artists who attempt an interpretation of Jesus. We hear this same attempt in music. Some of the most exalted music of the classical composers is music based on the events in the life of Jesus. Much of it was composed for use in church, some of it was not. All the special music for Christmas, Easter and other church holidays depends for part of its effect on the under-

Rembrandt (Dutch, 1606 – 1669), Christ with a Pilgrim's Staff
The Metropolitan Museum of Art, the Jules S. Bache Collection, 1949
Compare these two portraits of Jesus by the same artist. Why do you suppose they are different?

Rembrandt, Head of Christ
The Metropolitan Museum of Art, the Mr. and Mrs. Isaac D. Fletcher
  Collection. Bequest of Isaac D. Fletcher, 1917

standing of the listener as to what it is all about. The deep sorrow of Good Friday, the great exaltation of Easter, the joy of Christmas, all are expressed in music based on the New Testament. Again, not all the music based on the life of Jesus is classical, nor even always good. Think of all the Christmas carols, Easter carols, Negro spirituals, hymns, Gospel songs, hillbilly songs, which have as their theme one of the events in the life of Jesus, or express simply the deep appreciation of the writer for that life lived so long ago.

Historical Influence of Jesus

The comprehension of much of history depends on knowledge and understanding of the interpretations which men put upon the life and teachings of Jesus. How can one understand the Crusades, for example, with 200 years of fighting, all in a holy cause and all in the name of Jesus, unless one understands the fervor roused in human breasts by the sacred places in Palestine where Jesus walked? Christianity had developed considerably from the simple gospel of Jesus by the time of the Crusades, but it was, nevertheless, the religion founded on his teachings, and it was in his name that the knights rode forth to conquer the infidel and drive him from the sacred city.

The history of the Western world from the fall of Rome until the Reformation was dominated by the development of the Roman Catholic Church—the church which traces its history back to Jesus through its Popes. Peter, according to the Roman Catholic tradition, was the first Pope chosen by Jesus to head his church after he was gone. (Matthew 16:17-19). From Peter, according to this doctrine, the authority has been handed down through the centuries in unbroken succession to the present Pope. The policies and teachings of the

Roman Catholic Church helped mold the civilization which we now know as "Western."

In modern times the question of interpretation or evaluation of Christianity, whether it be Protestant, Roman Catholic, or Eastern Orthodox, colors much of our political history. In such issues as the election of an American president, the establishment of Communism, or the founding of the Irish Free State, the question of the interpretation of Christianity plays a mighty part. Indeed, the events which resulted in the early settlement of our country dramatically illustrate how important religious beliefs are in the minds of men. How different the history of our country would have been if New England had not been settled by Pilgrims and Puritans whose viewpoint and standards still permeate much of our culture!

Understanding Our Neighbors

To understand much of our neighbor's behavior, his attitudes and his way of life, we must understand our neighbor's religion. Each man's interpretation of those things which he thinks right or wrong depends on his learned religious values, whether he is conscious of the fact or not. To cite a trivial example, a Roman Catholic family may not have the same feeling about hanging out the laundry on a Sunday afternoon as would the family descended from New England Puritans. Attitudes toward more serious issues such as birth control, the use of alcohol, divorce and intermarriage, to name but a few, will, in essence, depend on the religious orientation of the family.

It is obvious, too, that in the same community customs differ widely from family to family. Consider the tremendous variety of customs celebrating Christmas and Easter.

To trace the origin of them all would be a major project. These holidays were originally festivals in connection with the change of the seasons. Christmas celebrated the winter solstice when the sun began its journey back toward the north bringing with it the lengthening of days and the promise of summer. Easter was the celebration of the vernal equinox when spring arrived and with it the resurrection of all the vegetation upon which man's very existence depended. Overlaid on these ancient celebrations is the Christian interpretation of the holidays. Mixed in with the very old traditions and customs are some newer ones which stem from the church's reinterpretation of the old customs in order to provide them with a Christian meaning.

The deep religious significance of these holidays is felt, not in the ancient celebration, although that affords us most of the fun and festivity, but in the expression of devotion to the events of the life of Jesus. One cannot grasp the essential meaning of these holidays without a knowledge of the events which they celebrate. Just knowing that Christmas celebrates the birth of Jesus and that Easter marks his resurrection is not enough to grasp the significance of these days for vast numbers of devout Christians. One must also understand the essence of the life which inspired their celebration.

There are many other examples from daily life which reflect the influence of the events in the life of that man who walked by the shores of the Sea of Galilee so many centuries ago. Many of our habitually used phrases, for example, are actually New Testament references: "A Judas," "Turn the other cheek," "Walk the second mile," "Building a house on sand," "A Good Samaritan," or "The lost sheep."

The accident of our being part of the Western world is reason enough for learning all we can about Jesus. When we make the effort and come into the presence of his personality through studying his life and teaching we shall understand better why he had the influence he did.

Chapter Three:

How Do We Know?

Have you ever witnessed an automobile accident? Did your teacher ever ask you to explain exactly how a fight in the school yard started? Have you, as you began to describe the accident or fight, disagreed completely about it with someone else who was also a witness and just as close to the scene as you were?

If you have, you know how hard it is to describe an event objectively. How much more difficult it is to describe a person's life! It should not surprise us that the New Testament accounts of Jesus' life are not in complete agreement, nor that later portrayers of him present such widely differing interpretations of what he was like.

Disagreement of witnesses is one of the difficult problems facing the courts where damage suits are brought. Who is right? Two or three witnesses tell different versions of the same accident. Each of the witnesses may be, and usually is, an honest, upright citizen. The discrepancies in the descriptions are not due to dishonesty, but to a real difference of opinion as to what actually happened. Where was the witness standing, for example? An automobile accident will seem to happen in one way to the person standing on the sidewalk, in another way to the person driving the car, and in still a third to the person who was hit. The physical position determines at what angle a witness sees the car as it strikes the pedestri-

Portrait of Christ, from Byzantine mosaic, late fifth or early sixth
century. Original in Archbishop's Palace, Ravenna. One of the
earliest portrayals.
The Metropolitan Museum of Art, Johnston Fund, 1924

an. Not only the physical position but also the mental attitude is important. Sometimes an attitude causes a person to think that he saw something which actually never happened. A witness may swear that he saw the pedestrian jump back just before the car hit him in an effort to avoid the accident, when, as a matter of fact, the car bumping the pedestrian was what made it appear that he had jumped. The witness, however, is so convinced that the accident was the fault of the driver of the car that he is sure this is what happened. He isn't lying. He is simply seeing the accident from a point of view. The point of view is both physical and mental. If he had been standing in a different spot he would have seen that his description was incorrect, or if he had had a different attitude he might have interpreted the accident differently.

Which Point of View?

If one is writing today about an event in the past, such as an event in the life of Jesus, the same limitations are present. In such writing the author has a point of view. He may gather all the material he can, try to check everything which has been written about it and do an admirable job of research. The fact remains that he is writing in the twentieth century. He has attitudes which belong to his time. He is looking back across the years at something which happened in a different age. Is it possible, then, for him to be completely accurate?

Even the meanings of words can change from one period to another. An example of this is seen in the change of words from the 1611 King James translation of the Bible to the 1946 Revised Standard Version of the New Testament. The word translated "charity" in I Corinthians 13 was changed to "love" because "love" today means more nearly what the Greek word meant in the first century. "Charity" today in the twentieth century has the meaning of "handouts," often without any feeling of compassion or concern; yet it was these latter ingredients which were implied by Paul in his letter to the Corinthians.

There is an added factor which causes trouble for the historical writer. That factor is the earlier interpreter of the event or person. A good historical writer tries to discover what the attitudes of the previous writers were so that it will be possible to counteract any bias which existed in the reporting of the event. This is a complicated process, probably never completely successful. When one is writing about events or people which affect religious belief, the task becomes still more difficult.

If an author firmly believes something, it is almost impossible for him to accept an idea which tends to throw doubt on that belief. Thus, he will see in the events or in the life of the person about whom he is writing only those facts which do not conflict with his firmly held religious beliefs. This same phenomenon can be seen in the evaluation of contemporary events or ideas as well. We can make this problem clear by looking at examples.

Galileo

Take the story of Galileo and the attitude of the Medieval church toward him. During the Middle Ages people believed that the earth was the center of the universe and that all the planets and the sun revolved around it. It was believed that man was the most important creation of God, which made it logical that man and his world should be the center of things. This theory had been set forth in the second century A.D. by an astronomer named Claudius Ptolemaeus who came from Alexandria, and so it became known as the Ptolemaic theory.

It was not until 1543 that a Polish astronomer, Copernicus, challenged this idea and proposed the theory that the planets and the earth revolved around the sun. He also suggested that the earth was not stationary as had been believed previously, but that it turned on its axis once every twenty-four hours. Today it is hard for us to believe that such an obvious truth should have been rejected by most who heard it. Yet it was rejected because it was against the religious beliefs of the majority of the people of the time. Of course there were some who accepted it, as there always are some in every time whose minds are open to receive new knowledge.

Soon there were two groups: those who held to the old Ptolemaic theory and those who adhered to the new Copernican theory. One of the latter was a brilliant scientist named Galileo Galilei who lived from 1564 to 1642, and who was one of the first men to use the newly invented telescope. He discovered many things about the planets, the moon and the stars which had been unknown before, and his findings convinced him of the truth of the Copernican theory. He was strongly opposed in these views, however, by representatives of the church and others who felt that their idea of the earth as the special creation of God was threatened by such teachings. Finally he was called before the Inquisition (the body appointed by the Roman Catholic Church to try heretics) after having been warned that he must not teach this new astronomy because it was undermining Christian belief and was in defiance of the church's teaching. He was forced to recant, to deny that he believed the Copernican theory. He did this, and was allowed to live.

In our twentieth-century eyes this seems like a strange tale. We have for so long accepted the Copernican theory that it is hard to believe that men were actually put to death for holding it. Our judgment of those who had refused to accept this new astronomy is likely to be harsh. Yet we must remember that the Ptolemaic theory had been held for thirteen centuries before Galileo. Thirteen hundred years is a long time. To change an idea that has been so firmly held over such a long period takes time and convincing. The church leadership of that era had believed sincerely that the earth was the center of the universe. Many of its teachings were built around that theory. If these teachings were true, then the earth *had* to be the center of the universe. To them it could not be otherwise.

On the other hand, we are likely to be scornful of Galileo, a scientist who was convinced in his own mind that what he was teaching was true, and yet capitulated to the demands of the church to deny what he really believed. Put yourself in his place. Consider his problem: choose to recant, or choose to be burned at the stake. If he recanted, he satisfied the authorities and would be able to live out his life doing his research which later generations would accept. It would take a brave man, or a foolhardy one, depending on your point of view, to choose the stake!

This episode helps us in our discussion of Jesus because it shows, in the first place, how religious belief sometimes clouds objective judgment. The church was in error in refusing to accept the Copernican theory, but in its own eyes it was right because it was defending religious faith which came before all else. In the second place, this episode illustrates for us how our own judgment is influenced by the standards which we hold. We can see this in our reaction to Galileo's recanting and to the church's condemnation of him. We might ask ourselves: with whom are we in sympathy as we read about this, and why?

The Dead Sea Scrolls

From our own time an example of how religious belief clouds objective judgment is seen in the controversy which raged about the Dead Sea Scrolls and their interpretation. In 1947 the discovery of ancient scrolls in a cave on the edge of the Dead Sea excited Biblical scholars when it became apparent that these scrolls had been hidden in the cave where they were found at a date not long after the time of Jesus. They were part of a library belonging to a group who lived in a nearby monastery. The building site was excavated later, and much was learned about the group who lived there.

The place is called Qumran and the group who lived there from about 110 B.C. to 68 A.D. were probably Essenes, of whom we will hear more later. Those particularly interested in the study of the New Testament were excited because they hoped that this discovery would throw some light on the time of Jesus, and therefore be helpful in interpreting the New Testament. Who could tell, perhaps there might even be something in this find which would come from Jesus, or from one of his followers? Those whose particular interest was in the Old Testament were thrilled to find a scroll of the book of Isaiah which was centuries earlier than any of the copies they had heretofore had. They would be able to check their translations and their interpretations with this really ancient manuscript. They, too, hoped that more scrolls would produce further help to them in their work. The New Testament scholars were destined to be disappointed because there have been no finds in the Dead Sea caves which throw any clear light on the figure of Jesus. The Old Testament students have received many manuscripts which have been of help to them. However, all those interested in the life and time of Jesus have received much new material which helps in understanding the period in which he lived. The great controversy has been over the interpretation of this material.

At first, discussion of these scrolls was limited to those who were actually in the field of Biblical research. The public at large knew little about them, if they had read the newspaper accounts of these finds at all. In 1955 the discovery of the scrolls was brought to the attention of the public by a man who was not a Biblical scholar but a literary critic named Edmund Wilson, writing in *The New Yorker*. He told the story of the finding of the scrolls, and he made some suggestions as to the importance which they might have in the interpretation of the words of Jesus. Immediately, there was a great furor. On the one hand, there were those who felt that any questioning of the traditional view which had been held of Jesus and his teaching through the centuries was not permissible. These were people who, like the Roman Catholic Church of the sixteenth century, knew what they believed and would not accept anything which threatened that belief. They insisted that the Dead Sea Scrolls could not show us anything at all about Jesus. At the other extreme, there were those who hoped that this find would tell us a great deal about Jesus so that the traditional view of him as the Son of God could be disproved. These people made extravagant claims for the importance of the scrolls, often reading into their interpretation meanings which are not really there.

As one might expect, the true significance of the scrolls lies somewhere in between these two extreme positions. As more and more of the manuscripts were unrolled and read, new light was thrown on both the Old and the New Testaments.

The greatest contribution which this discovery made to Biblical studies was that it revealed much about a group which hitherto had been almost unknown. This group was living on the shores of the Dead Sea during the lifetime of Jesus and of John the Baptist, and for a while during the earliest period of Christianity. It would be strange indeed if it had had no influence on Jesus nor on early Christianity. To understand the Qumran sect is to understand a school of thought which made up part of the background of Jesus, even though it is not mentioned by name in the New Testament. From understanding this sect we receive help in interpreting some of the phrases, teachings and events in the Gospels themselves. We must not exaggerate the importance of the scrolls, but we must not overlook it either; and we must not be afraid to change some of our ideas about Jesus should prove come out of further studies which might make this necessary.

Suppose that in some as yet unexplored cave, there comes definite proof that Jesus had spent his childhood in the monastery at Qumran. There is, of course, no evidence that this is so. There probably never will be. But suppose that this happened. How do you think people would react? Would they destroy all the children's books about the boy Jesus helping in his father's carpenter shop? Do you think that somewhere in folklore or legend that the story of Jesus, the carpenter's son, would still persist?

The argument about the Dead Sea Scrolls shows us that, even today, religious beliefs influence judgments. Each time a discovery is made which bears on religion, deeply held beliefs will influence the interpretations given it. Is it possible to escape this bias?

Facts versus Theories

How can we ever distinguish truth from biased interpretation? Fact from theory? Sometimes this is quite simple. More often it is difficult, even impossible. To go back to our automobile accident for a moment, the police will question witnesses and will listen to all they have to say. However, they will also apply other means to discover the truth about the responsibility for an accident. They might take out their tape measures to measure the distance from the collision to the place where the brakes were first applied. If they found that the car had not been braked at a distance which enabled it to stop in time, the guilt would be established. It would be proved that the driver was negligent. This, then, would be a fact.

31

Head of Christ, from roundel, beginning of sixteenth century
The Metropolitan Museum of Art, gift of J. Pierpont Morgan, 1916

More often, however, it will be a combination of facts and theory which will determine the guilt. In a jury trial, for example, all the facts are placed before the jury. They listen to the witnesses and hear the reports. It then falls on them to determine what the truth is and to act upon it. Many factors come into play: do the witnesses seem to be telling the truth? Does anyone of them have prejudices which should make his testimony suspect? Does anyone of them have a physical handicap which might affect his reliability? After all the evidence is heard, it is then up to the jury to determine what happened. By comparing impressions and evaluations, a jury sincerely attempting to find out the truth usually arrives at it. It is still possible that they may be wrong. At a later date, perhaps, further evidence might be turned up which could reverse their decision. However, with the facts as they had them, their decision is as good as any could be. In other words, they have propounded a theory, based on evidence, of who was responsible for the accident.

Facts, then, are those phenomena which can be proved. Theories are those explanations of phenomena which cannot be proved. Much of what we call history is theory. There are a few facts: events we know happened, dates on which they happened, people we know lived. If we go beyond a mere listing of these facts into any attempt to explain them, we are in the realm of theory. Since all writing about history is the attempt to interpret facts, to give some meaning to them, history writing is theory. It may be sound theory in the sense that a great many people agree that this is a logical interpretation of the event, but it is theory nevertheless. As we read history, we need to bear these things in mind. We must sort out the facts from the interpretation insofar as we can. We need to evaluate the interpretation, taking into account whose it is, eliminating the interpreter's bias as much as we can, and then reconstruct our own interpretation of known facts on the basis of what seems reasonable to us.

There are other occasions when we see the results of facts,

rather than the facts themselves. Theories are then built around the known result in order to explain the cause of it. This can be seen in the realm of natural law. There are some things which happen. For example, a tree topples over. It is observed that when the wind blows, the tree for which the wind is too strong will fall. We do not see the wind, but we know that it exists because we feel it and see its results. But what causes the wind? From the time of primitive man there have been theories concerning this. Today we have our scientific explanation of wind as the air movements over the surface of the earth, but exactly what causes them or how they are caused is still in the theoretical stage.

The same is true of our reading of history. Sometimes we see the results of an historical event, but we do not know what its cause was. Nor do we know all we wish to know about it. When we look at Christianity, we see a centuries-old religion. We know when it started, we see the results of its having started, but we have many interpretations of how these results came to be. The consensus is, however, that a fact stands behind this development. That fact is a man named Jesus. To understand Christianity we have to find out all we can about him—who he was, what he was like, what he thought.

Fact and Theory about Jesus

How are we going to know what is true and what is not true about Jesus? All that we have learned about fact and theory will be important here. We must go to what sources we have and find there any facts that we can. We must then interpret these facts as best we can. We will be reading what others have written so that at times sorting out fact from interpretation will be difficult. But we must try to do this. We must also be careful that what we are reading in the Gospel record is not being read into it by ourselves, because of our own point of view. When we have finished, you will have a theory concerning Jesus. That theory will be based on surprisingly few facts. It will have the strength of being your own, based on your own research, but it will have the weaknesses all theories have, and you must stand ready to change it should some better theory come your way.

Chapter Four:
Gospels and Gospel Writers

Matthew, Mark and Luke, the first three books of the New Testament, are our main sources for a study of the life and teachings of Jesus. John, the fourth Gospel, is quite different from the first three and is not considered historically reliable. We will consider the reasons for this judgment of John after we have looked at the first three Gospel writers. Who were the men who wrote these books? Did they know Jesus? Where did they gather their material? What were their reasons for writing about him? Are their books reliable as a source of information about Jesus? How can we learn the facts about the man whose life we are seeking to understand? These are a few of the questions which occur to us as we look to the New Testament for help in our study.

The Synoptics—Alike and Different

If we read the first three books of the New Testament carefully, we will note both similarities and differences among them. Because of the obvious similarities they are called the *Synoptics* or "look alikes." Scholars have taken these three Gospels and arranged them in columns so that they may be

Christ in Majesty, with symbols of four Gospel writers in the corners,
from lectionary, vicinity of Halle Saxony, before 1245
Courtesy of the Pierpont Morgan Library

compared easily. One Gospel, usually Mark, is taken in its present order and then all the parallel passages from Matthew and Luke are arranged across the page. You might like to look at one of these books. They are called *Harmonies* because they "harmonize" the three Gospels. When a comparison is made, several things become evident. The simple fact stands out that Mark is the shortest of the three. Closer observation will show that all three follow the same order in telling of tne events in the life of Jesus. This is known as the narrative. We can also observe that there are events told by Matthew and Luke which are not in Mark, and that there are events found only in Matthew or Luke. There is very little found only in Mark. The same could be said for the sayings and parables which we call the teaching. And when we look at the teaching in all three Gospels, we will find that although the wording of the parables and sayings is usually identical, or similar, that the setting in which they are given varies from Gospel to Gospel. Why is this?

Let us travel, in imagination, back to the first century. We live in a small town in Galilee. One morning, as we are in the market place, one of our neighbors asks us whether we have heard the teaching of a man from a village not far from the one in which we live. The neighbor tells us that he is an inspired speaker. His name is Jesus and he was baptized by John the Baptist in the River Jordan. At that time, so the story goes, he was so impressed with his experience of baptism that he decided that he, too, must preach. Now that John the Baptist is in prison, many of John's disciples have joined the disciples of Jesus and are listening to him at every opportunity. As you hear your neighbor's enthusiastic report of the great inspiration he had received from listening to this itinerant preacher, you decide that you must seek him out. Since he will be preaching in the immediate vicinity within a day or two, you decide to go with some of your friends to hear him.

This is the first century, and you live in a small town, so books are almost unknown to you. You have seen the scroll of the Law in the local synagogue, and you have sat for hours in the courtyard of the synagogue listening to the rabbi expound that Law to you. You have had to learn long passages from it and from the Prophets. The rabbi recited it to you, and then you and all the others repeated the passage after him until you knew it by heart. You have never learned to read and write, but you have thought much about religious matters because of the teaching you have received in this manner. Your interest is much aroused by the tales concerning this Jesus who seems to be becoming so popular.

On a hot, dusty day you and your friends proceed to a grove of trees between your town and the next where you see a man seated, surrounded by a small group of men whom you surmise are probably his disciples. Around this little group, standing in a circle, are dozens of men, women and children listening intently as the man speaks. You and your friends move in as close as you can, straining to hear every word.

Now, imagine that you are back home again and that you are repeating Jesus' words to a friend who had not gone with you. You had listened to him talk for a half hour or more. Everything you remember has to be in your head because you could not take notes on any of it. Would you remember word for word everything he said? How much do you think you *would* remember of that half hour's talk? When you and your friends discuss the talk the next day, how much of that half hour do you think you, among you, would be able to reconstruct?

Suppose thirty years have passed since you had this experience of hearing Jesus speak. Not long after you heard him he was crucified. His followers are now anxious to learn all that they can of what he had said because they are beginning to forget it. The figure of Jesus has become central in a new religion called Christianity, and its followers deem every word which he had spoken as precious. One of these Christians comes to see you and to ask you what you remember from that day long ago when you heard Jesus speak. How much do you think you would remember? Suppose you had heard Jesus on several different occasions. How accurate do you think your memory would be as to what he said on which occasion?

The Differences Among the Gospels

This excursion into imagination illustrates the theory which has been set forth by scholars to explain some of the differences among the Gospels. What was remembered by those who had heard Jesus were those things which had particularly impressed them and which were easily remembered. Short sayings, which were the "punch lines" of what were originally much longer talks, and parables, which were stories, were easily remembered. The setting in which these sayings and parables were spoken was forgotten. Then as the Christian church began to grow, those who were preaching in the church felt the need to have the words of Jesus. What they remembered was not enough. Therefore, collections of sayings and parables were made for use in the early Christian church. The need for these collections became more urgent as those who had actually seen and heard Jesus began to die and the preaching was being done by those who had never personally seen or heard him.

Eventually, the need was felt to have a written account of the life and teaching of Jesus and so our Gospels came into being. They were not written by eyewitnesses to the events which they describe. The authors had to rely on the collections which had been made before them. Perhaps the Gospels we now have were not the first to have been written, but were the ones which survived.

Scholars are not completely agreed on the details of this theory, but it is generally accepted that the Gospels were written with the needs of the early Christian church in mind. For example, the source which Matthew and Luke relied on for the material which is not found in Mark is called Q for *Quelle*, which is a German word which means simply "source." Some hold that this was a pre-Gospel gospel. In other words, they believe that it was a work similar to those we have, but of earlier date and now lost. Others feel that this so-called gospel was a number of sources and that Matthew and Luke happened to choose the same ones in some instances, but in others chose different ones. Again, Mark is usually assumed to be the earliest Gospel, so the simplest explanation for the appearance of the same material in all three Gospels is that Matthew and Luke took this similar material from Mark. However, it is possible that all three relied on a common source or sources.

Whatever the details of the theory concerning the writing of our present Gospels it is vital that we remember they were not eyewitness, word for word reports; and that we recognize that many changes took place in the material about Jesus before it ever came to be written down. What about those who wrote our Gospels? What manner of men were they? What motivated them to write "biographies" of Jesus? Who were they? When did they write?

The Writer of Mark

The Gospel which bears this name has traditionally been credited to John Mark, one of the early Christians who is mentioned in the Book of Acts (Acts 12:12 and 25; 13:5), and in the Epistles of Paul (Colossians 4:10; Philemon 24), as well as in the Epistle of I Peter (5:13). A tradition which can be traced back to the second century tells us that Peter went to Rome where he founded the Christian church in that

Mark, with his symbol of a lion, from The Four Gospels with Prefaces,
early twelfth century English manuscript
Courtesy of the Pierpont Morgan Library

city and that he was joined there by Paul. The Book of Acts tells us that Paul did go to Rome, but there, tantalizingly, the book ends! Tradition further asserts that both Peter and Paul were martyred in the infamous persecution of the Christians under the Emperor Nero in A.D. 64. Theory about the authorship of the Gospel suggests that John Mark went to Rome with Peter, perhaps as his interpreter, and that after the death of Peter he wrote down a chronicle of the life of Jesus so that the church there would have it as a guide. The need for this was felt by the people in the church at this time since their leaders lost their lives in the persecution. This would date the Gospel around the year A.D. 70 or a little earlier or later.

This is an attractive theory which must be accepted with caution. It is obvious, for example, that the Gospel is not the "reminiscences of Peter the Disciple." It includes some much later material which bears the mark of the early church too clearly to have been contemporary with Jesus. There are also sections which show evidence of having gone through the process, which we discussed in the previous section, of being passed on by word of mouth for a length of time before being written down. In short, scholars can neither prove nor disprove this theory about the authorship of the Gospel, but they are reasonably sure that whoever the author was, he used several sources. One of these sources might well have been the preaching and teaching of Peter.

There are some characteristics of the Gospel of Mark which you can check for yourself. Here are these characteristics, followed by references. These are not all the references. As you read the Gospel, you will find others. It would be a good idea just to read this Gospel all the way through as though it were a story you were reading for the first time. Mark is a good Gospel to read this way, if only because one of its characteristics is that it is the shortest! And it is probably the earliest we possess.

The author of this Gospel was directing his book toward

those who were not Jewish (Mark 5:41; 7:3-4; 7:34; 15:34).

He thought of Jesus as having human characteristics. Compare the following passages with their parallels in the other Gospels. What has dropped out of the Markan version in each case? What have the other Gospels dropped out?

Mark 3: 1-6 (Matthew 12: 9-14; Luke 6:5-11).

Mark 7: 31-35 (Matthew 15: 29-31).

Mark 10:13-16 (Matthew 19:13-15; Luke 18:15-17).

He believed that Jesus was specially chosen by God (Mark 1:11; 8:29; 9:7; 14: 61-62), but that Jesus tried to keep this a secret (Mark 1:40-45; 5:43; 7:36; 8: 29-30; 9:9). This is Mark's explanation as to why everyone did not have faith in Jesus. This "secrecy doctrine" is found in other Gospels in the material which is based on Mark, or the Markan sources.

The Writer of Matthew

The Gospel of Matthew bears the name of one of the lesser known Disciples. Traditionally Matthew is supposed to have written it, but scholars agree that he could not have done so. The author was probably familiar with Mark, since he used most of it in his Gospel. Or he might have been familiar, not with the Gospel of Mark, but with the Markan source. If he had been an eyewitness to the events he described, would he have borrowed so widely from an earlier piece of work? He also used other sources including some of the collections of sayings and teachings which were made earlier than the time of the written Gospels.

Who was the author of the Gospel if Matthew, the publican, did not write it? We will probably never know with certainty who he was, but we can look at his Gospel and learn a few things about him. If we read Matthew, even superficial-

Matthew, with his symbol of a man, from The Four Gospels with
  Prefaces, early twelfth century English manuscript
Courtesy of the Pierpont Morgan Library

ly, we shall notice that the author takes great pains to show that throughout the life of Jesus the Old Testament prophecies were being fulfilled by him. We can see, too, that the author thinks of Jesus as the long-awaited Messiah, or Savior, whose coming had been predicted in the Old Testament. He uses what are called proof texts to show this. In other words, he takes a passage from the Old Testament and shows how an event he is describing fulfills it. The quoting of the Old Testament verse "proves" that the event described has been predicted. Some examples of this can be found in Matthew 3:3; 4:12-16; 8:17; 12:17-21; 13:14-15; 21:4-7. In this last reference, do you think that the author has interpreted the Old Testament passage correctly?

If we look for the human qualities in Jesus which we found in Mark, the evidence of emotion, or having to *try* to perform a miracle, we shall find them gone. This change may be because the Gospel is later than Mark so that the idea of Jesus as a man specially related to God and, therefore, not like other men, was more widely held and clearer in men's minds than at the time of Mark. Or it may have been because of the particular idea of Jesus which the author, himself, had.

The arrangement of the Gospel is different from the other two in that it is carefully organized. Jesus is presented as a great teacher and interpreter of the Jewish Law. There are five major discourses in Matthew: the Sermon on the Mount, 5-7; the charge to the Disciples, 10; a collection of parables, 13; sayings on brotherhood, 18; and sayings concerning the end of the world, 24-25. This arrangement was obviously made by the author because, although there is much material included in these discourses which is peculiar to Matthew, there are also many sayings and parables which are found in the other Gospels in different contexts. It is probably because Matthew included so much teaching that the Gospel became so popular and thus was placed first in the New Testament.

Who was the author of Matthew? We can piece together a few things about him. He was thoroughly familiar with the

Old Testament and so we may assume that he was born Jewish. However, he was a follower of Jesus and wrote his Gospel to spread the message of Jesus; therefore, he had become a Christian. He must have belonged to the group which we call Jewish Christians. This group would include, of course, all of the Disciples as well as many more converts. The distinction was made in the early years of the movement to differentiate such Christians from those who were Greek-speaking and non-Jewish. Matthew wrote for the Jews. We surmise this from the fact that he went to such pains to prove that Jesus was the Messiah foretold in the Old Testament. This "proof" would mean nothing to a non-Jew. Scholars have also surmised that Matthew wrote his Gospel about the year A.D. 80 in Antioch in Syria which was one of the important centers of Christianity in the first century and which had a large Jewish population. The reason for the writing of the Gospel would seem to be to add to the meager outline of the life of Jesus as presented by Mark a larger selection of the teachings of Jesus. This inclusion of so much of the teaching is the important and main contribution of Matthew to our knowledge of Jesus. If we had only the teaching contained in Mark, we would know much less about what Jesus taught.

The Writer of Luke

The Gospel of Luke bears the name of a companion of Paul who is called in Colossians 4:14 "the beloved physician," and who is mentioned again in Philemon 24. Luke is also presumed to be the author of Acts, which tells what happened after the death of Jesus. The fact that Acts is Volume Two of Luke is obscured by the insertion of the Gospel of John between the two in our New Testament. Look at Luke 1:1-4 and at Acts 1:1. If Luke was really the author of Acts,

Luke, with his symbol of an ox, from The Four Gospels with Prefaces,
early twelfth century English manuscript
Courtesy of the Pierpont Morgan Library

and there is no evidence to show that he was not, then he traveled with Paul on some of his journeys and had the opportunity to meet some of the eyewitnesses to the events of Jesus' life. This surmise is made from the fact that there are included in the book of Acts four "we" passages which switch from the third person to the first. These are found in Acts 16: 10-17; 20: 5-15; 21:1-18; 27:1-28:16.

From the introduction to Luke we would assume that Luke was a Gentile (not a Jew) and that his main interest was in writing the story of Jesus for the Greek-speaking Gentiles. The fact that the chronology of the Gospel is linked to the imperial chronology of Rome gives further strength to this point of view, as does the fact that Jesus is placed in a less limited setting than in Matthew. This can be seen by a comparison of the birth stories in Matthew and in Luke.

As one reads the Gospel of Luke the skill of the writer becomes evident. Where Mark is short, to the point, but rather flat-footed in its presentation of Jesus, and Matthew is carefully organized to the point of seeming contrived, Luke is a beautifully written narrative. In Mark we see the human, lifelike qualities of Jesus, and in Matthew we see Jesus as a teacher. In Luke the emphasis is on the sympathy and compassion of Jesus, his interest in the lowly and downtrodden as in Luke 14: 12-13; 7:13 or in the beautiful parable of the Good Samaritan, Luke 10: 29-37. The Gospel of Luke also contains many more references to women than the other two Gospels. It is in this book that we learn the names of some of the women followers of Jesus (Luke 8:13). In short, it is evident that Luke wrote for those who might be converted to Christianity from among the Gentiles. Therefore, he included in his Gospel those things about Jesus which would appeal especially to them, and he emphasized the fact that nothing Jesus did was anti-Roman.

He does not emphasize the fulfillment of Jewish prophecy as did Matthew. On the contrary, he attempted to place Jesus in a more universal setting to show that he was Savior for all, not just a select few. This probably explains his inclusion of so many references to Samaritans, women, the downtrodden —all people who were not included in the religious activities of the day. The Gospel of Luke probably had an influence in spreading Christianity to the slaves and the women of the Roman world, for in it they found a place for themselves. It is not known where this Gospel was written, nor when, but it is thought to date from about the year A.D. 90.

The Reliability of the Synoptics

Now that we have looked in some detail at the three Synoptic Gospels, we are in a position to evaluate them, and to ask some questions about their reliability as our source for learning about the life and teachings of Jesus. Bearing in mind our discussion in Chapter Three on the importance of recognizing that all history is written from a point of view, summarize the point of view from which each of the Gospel writers looked at the life of Jesus. What specific ideas did each have which might influence his interpretation of Jesus?

To prepare ourselves more fully for the study of the Gospels, we must, of course, learn what we can about the background against which they were written. We must learn something about the historical events from the time immediately preceding the birth of Jesus through the era during which the Gospels were written. We need to know what religious ideas the people of the time held, and what kind of life they led. Obviously we are going to have only a glimpse of these things. We shall select those events and ideas which have the greatest bearing on our understanding of Jesus. First, however, we must pause to look at the Gospel of John, the Fourth Gospel, which we have not thus far included in our study. What is its value to us?

The Writer of John

The Gospel of John is unlike the first three Gospels in style, in content and in the picture of Jesus which it draws. A glance at the first chapter, or one at random in the Gospel, will show even the most casual reader that here is a work which is not of the same type as the Synoptics. Yet the Gospel of John is probably more widely read than any of the others. Why is this? Perhaps it is because the book is so beautifully written and so well phrased. It is a book which is not intended to be read literally, or to be factual, but rather it is a great work of symbolism and of interpretation. The picture of Jesus which is drawn in it is not that of a human being, but rather of a being who has existed through eternity and who has come to earth briefly in order to show men how to have faith so that he may be united with God.

"In the beginning was the Word, and the Word was with God, and the Word was God. He was in the beginning with God; all things were made through him, and without him was not anything made that was made. In him was life, and the life was the light of men. The light shines in the darkness, and the darkness has not overcome it." John 1:1-5

"And the Word became flesh and dwelt among us, full of grace and truth; we have beheld his glory, glory as of the only Son from the Father." John 1:14

"The next day he saw Jesus coming toward him, and said 'Behold, the Lamb of God, who takes away the sin of the world.' " John 1:29

"He who comes from above is above all; he who is of the earth belongs to the earth, and of the earth he speaks; he who comes from heaven is above all. He bears witness to what he has seen and heard, yet no one receives his testimony; he who receives his testimony sets his seal to this, that God is true. For he whom God has sent utters the words of God, for it is not by measure that he gives the Spirit; the

John, with his symbol of an eagle, from The Four Gospels with
Prefaces, early twelfth century English manuscript
Courtesy of the Pierpont Morgan Library

Father loves the Son, and has given all things into his hand. He who believes in the Son has eternal life; he who does not obey the Son shall not see life, but the wrath of God rests upon him." John 3: 31-36

"Jesus said to them, 'I am the bread of life; he who comes to me shall not hunger, and he who believes in me shall never thirst.' " John 6:35

"Again Jesus spoke to them saying, 'I am the light of the world; he who follows me will not walk in darkness, but will have the light of life.' John 8:12

"Let not your hearts be troubled; believe in God, believe also in me. In my Father's house are many rooms; if it were not so, would I have told you that I go to prepare a place for you? And when I go and prepare a place for you, I will come again and will take you to myself, that where I am you may be also." John 14:1-3

Some have called John the Spiritual Gospel because it is so full of imagery. This makes it hard to date. Therefore, it is impossible to determine its authorship. The traditional author is the Disciple John. The Gospel itself implies that it was written by him (John 21: 20-24). Yet, because of the difficult ideas in this book, modern scholars have tended to think that the Gospel was not written by John, but that it is of a much later period. They have felt that considerable time must have elapsed between the death of Jesus and the advanced theological ideas which are reflected in this Gospel. The date which has been widely accepted is the first part of the second century, usually about A.D. 110.

However, the discovery of the Dead Sea Scrolls has made a re-evaluation of this Gospel necessary. There are ideas in the Gospel which are found also in the scrolls. Some of the language of John sounds much like that in some of the scrolls. Since the monastery at Qumran was destroyed in A.D. 68, it is obvious that these ideas were prevalent much earlier than had previously been thought. It may be that the Gospel which we have thought for a long time was the latest of the four may indeed be contemporary with or earlier than the Synoptics. For our study of the life and teachings of Jesus, we will confine ourselves to the Synoptic Gospels. Whenever we do look at John, we should remember that whatever the date and whoever the author, the Gospel is more like a glorious hymn of praise than a story of a man's life. If it is the life we want to learn about, rather than the effect it had on one poet, we must study the Synoptics.

Chapter Five:

Facts From the Past Which Help

Pharisees, Sadducees, Messiah, Kingdom of God—what do these terms mean? Can we understand the Gospels without knowing? Will a simple definition of each be sufficient? Even a superficial reading of the Gospels will show us that we need more than definitions to help us understand them. We need to move back into the centuries preceding the birth of Jesus in order to see what events produced the groups and the ideas which play such an important part in the Gospel story and in the formation of the thought of Jesus.

Alexander the Great and Hellenism

Do you remember reading about Alexander, the Greek ruler who was called "The Great"? It is hard to believe that the influence of this man who lived in the fourth century B.C. could have extended so far that it molded the times in which Jesus lived. But such is the case.

Alexander almost accomplished his aim in life which was to conquer the entire known world and make of it a vast empire in which Greek civilization prevailed. His leadership was strong, his armies were powerful and he swept before him country after country until he made most of the eastern world a part of his empire. He even penetrated as far as the border of India. On the way back from India Alexander the Great's dream crumbled after a career of only thirteen years, for he caught a fever and died in Babylon in 323 B.C. at the age of just thirty-three. His ambition to make the whole world Greek influenced the course of the entire Near East for centuries in spite of his relatively short life. How did this happen?

After Alexander's death a struggle ensued among his generals over who would be Alexander's successor. One of the generals named Antigonus was able to keep the leadership until his death, but only by waging many bloody battles. After his death the empire fell into three parts, each headed by one general. They continued to battle each other for control of more territory. Palestine stood between two of these empires, the Ptolemaic to the south which included Egypt, and the Seleucid to the north which included Asia Minor. As the two battled each other their armies marched back and forth across Palestine. At one point the Jews were subject to Ptolemy, and the next moment they were ruled by the conqueror from the north. Eventually, but not until 198 B.C., the Seleucids succeeded in maintaining their control of Palestine.

The political history of this period is not too important to our understanding of the New Testament, but the cultural changes which were taking place are. Alexander the Great wanted to make the whole world Greek, not just in name, but in culture as well. He wanted Greek to be the universal language, Greek religion to be the universal religion and Greek customs to become those of everyone. His successors felt just as strongly about this. Their method was to form Greek colonies and to encourage Greeks to settle in the countries which they had conquered so that they might introduce all forms of Greek culture.

It is important to realize that the Greek culture which Alexander wished to introduce was not that of the greatest period of Greek civilization. The days of Homer, Socrates and Plato, Praxiteles and Aristophanes were over. The great Greek culture was beginning to decline. Moreover, it was impossible to introduce pure Greek culture into an alien land and keep it undiluted. The alien added its own imprint to the Greek. What emerged was the Hellenistic, not classic, Greek culture. This was Hebrew, Egyptian or Syrian culture with some of the externals of Greek culture laid on it. Much of the religion the people really did not want or understand, so that it became mechanical. Old values were undermined, resulting in moral confusion. Greek language changed as it absorbed expressions, phrases and pronunciations from the native tongues it was attempting to replace.

There were many in every area conquered by Alexander who opposed this attempt to "modernize" them. In Palestine many of the younger people, as elsewhere, began to adopt Greek customs and language to the horror of their more conservative elders. The adoption of Hellenism by large numbers of people led to the formation of two parties: those who were Hellenizers and those who opposed Hellenization. The Hellenistic party contained not only those who found the Greek culture pleasing to them and those who wanted to be modern and up-to-date, but it also included those who were politically ambitious, who wanted to be "in" with the ruler. In the latter group were many religious leaders who felt that the adaptation of the old ways to the new was possible and practical. If one had to live under a conqueror, they reasoned, one might as well get along with him.

On the other hand, opposing strenuously the infiltration of a pagan culture were those who believed in holding to the traditional ways of the Jewish people, particularly in religious matters. They feared absorption into the Greek patterns to the point where there would no longer be any Jewish culture or religion. There were also those who felt that the way to freedom was not in compromise with the conqueror, but in maintaining independence in every possible way.

The fears of these "traditionalists" might well have been realized except for an accident of history. A ruler arose who did not know how to rule without creating so much antagonism that revolt was inevitable. His name was Antiochus Epiphanes. Epiphanes means "God made manifest" which is an indication of his arrogant attitude. Some of the unscrupulous leaders among the Jews bargained with him for appointment to high offices and actually assisted him in his mania for imposing his will on the people. He was an ardent Hellenizer and set about to make everything, even the Jewish religion, Greek. He identified the Jewish God with Zeus and set up temples throughout Palestine for the worship of Greek deities. Many of the Greek practices and even fashions were introduced, among them Greek games, a custom particularly distasteful to the faithful Jews because the Greeks played without clothes. Beneath the surface revolt seethed more violently with each new defilement of Jewish religion.

In 170 B.C. war broke out between Egypt and Antiochus, again over the issue of control of Palestine. While Antiochus was away at the battlefront, a rumor reached Jerusalem that he had been killed. The hated leader was dead! Revolt flared up. The anti-Hellenistic Jews were on the side of the Egyptians in their sympathies because they looked to Egypt to free them from the oppression which they felt under Antiochus. They attacked the Hellenizers, cleansed the Temple (the center of Jewish worship which was located in Jerusalem) and slaughtered many. Antiochus was, however, very much alive. He returned to Jerusalem, looted the Temple of anything left in it of value and began a persecution of those who were anti-Hellenizers. He forbade the practice of the Jewish religion on pain of death and attempted to force everyone to take part in the pagan rites which he had instituted. In 168

B.C. he erected a statue of Zeus in the Temple and, legend tells us, sacrificed a pig on the altar. To the faithful these were the last abominations. Jewish law strictly forbids the making of an image, and the pig is considered an unclean animal even for human consumption, let alone for a sacred sacrifice. Revolt was inevitable.

In the hills outside Jerusalem, a priest named Mattathias gathered around him his five sons and a few other men to plot the revolt. Soon they were joined by others, all determined to end the religious oppression. It seemed a suicidal thing to do. Antiochus had the strength of armies with him. What could a small band do against him? Nevertheless, they waged guerrilla warfare against the hated oppressor. Within a few months Mattathias died and his son Judas took over the leadership of the band. He was nicknamed "the hammerer," and his followers were called the Maccabees which means "hammerers." In 165 B.C. his revolt was miraculously successful. The Temple was cleansed of its alien elements, the pagan altars were removed and it was rededicated to the religion of the God of Israel. This event is still celebrated in Jewish homes today on the holiday called Hanukka. Judas' success was not entirely due to his skilled leadership, nor to the fanatic devotion of his followers, but in large part to the fact that there were rebellions in other parts of Antiochus' kingdom which called him away from Palestine. Garrisons continued to be maintained in Jerusalem, and warfare broke out sporadically for many years between the Syrian forces and the Jewish rebels. It was not until 142 B.C., some years after the death of both Antiochus and Judas, that Simon, the last of the Maccabee brothers, succeeded in securing complete independence for Palestine.

The Independent Years

The history of the next eighty years of Jewish history is exceedingly complicated. Since the independence of the Jewish people had been achieved in the name of religion and in a struggle which aimed at preserving religious freedom, the roles of the religious leader, or high priest, and the political leader, or king, became very confused, so that in some instances the roles were one and the same. Desire for political conquest and for power often outweighed religious principles. In the struggle to maintain control of the country many murders and assassinations were carried out; sometimes the "king" even killed all the members of his own family who might dispute his claim to rule! It was a bloody and distressed period.

By 64 B.C. two brothers were waging war over which one would be ruler. At this point the Roman power from the west was extending its rule over much of the Mediterranean world. One of Rome's illustrious generals, Pompey, was in the east waging a campaign to conquer more territory. The two brothers appealed to him to settle their dispute as to who should rule. Pompey was delighted to oblige, although Palestine itself was unimportant to Rome. Since it was a corridor between Egypt on the south and Asia Minor on the north, the conquest of these two far larger and wealthier areas would automatically place Palestine in a position where she would have to capitulate to any demand Rome made. However, to have her volunteer to be conquered was a pleasant surprise for Pompey. He acted quickly, settling the dispute by seizing Palestine himself. The Jewish nation came to an end, for Palestine was now subject to Rome.

The Roman Rule

It was the policy of Rome to establish native rulers in the territories which she conquered. Wisely, little interference was made by Roman authorities in the internal affairs of countries. So in Palestine the high priest was left to govern as before with the new title of ethnarch of Judea. He was, however, subject to Rome, and Palestine had to pay tribute to her. The conquests of territory made during the Maccabean period which did not really belong in the Jewish state at all because of differences in culture and religion, were added to Syria under a Roman governor. It was this governor to whom the high priest was responsible.

For a few years there was peace in Palestine, but not for long. The feuds between the claimants to the high priesthood continued with plots and counterplots, murders and revolts. The situation was further complicated by the fact that civil war broke out in Rome, a civil war which lasted for twenty years and ended in the rule of Julius Caesar. During these years a clever and ambitious statesman named Herod Antipater took advantage of the rivalries and the feuds to create for himself a position of considerable power. Antipater was an Idumaean, which meant that he was from the ancient land of Edom and therefore a follower of Judaism, but one who was not acceptable to the strict Jew because he was of racially mixed blood. When Julius Caesar came into power, Antipater was rewarded for his efforts by being made the governor of Judea in the hope that this would bring peace to the territory again. Antipater appointed two of his sons as officials in Jerusalem and Galilee. It is the latter, named Herod, in whom we are most interested.

Herod the Great

Herod, or Herod I, or Herod the Great, as he was known, was appointed by Octavius to be king of Judea in 40 B.C. after the death of his father who was poisoned as he was feasting with the high priest! Herod had difficulty in assuming office, however, for Palestine had once again been conquered, this time by the Parthians of Persia who had deposed the high priest, cut off his ears (making it impossible for him ever to serve again since maimed men were not allowed by Jewish law to be high priests) and sent him into exile. Herod had been in Rome receiving his appointment as "king of the Jews." When he returned to Palestine the Roman legions made short work of the Parthians, but Jewish opposition to Herod was more difficult to overcome. It took three years to do this and it was only accomplished superficially and with great bloodshed. Galilee was one of the sections in which there was the heaviest resistance. Jerusalem was another.

Finally, however, Herod managed to establish himself as the absolute ruler of Judea. He then appointed a high priest and set about governing his territory. He was one of the ablest rulers the Jewish people ever had. The Romans realized his ability and this was undoubtedly why they appointed him to the job of keeping peace in Palestine. He was, however, hated vehemently by the Jews. They disliked having any secular ruler in a position of power greater than that of the religious leader, the high priest. Under Herod the high priest was appointed by him, and, therefore, Herod had the greater power. He was also a Hellenizer and, although he was too wise a ruler to impose his Hellenism by force on the people, he encouraged it in many ways, chiefly through building temples and public buildings in the Greek manner. He rebuilt the Temple in Jerusalem for the Jewish people and did it lavishly. He did not deliberately offend the religious sensibilities of those whom he governed as had Antiochus Epiphanes, for example. Nevertheless, he was hated. He was an Oriental despot who did not hesitate to murder even members of his own family to achieve his ends. He was of mixed blood, and tyranny combined with racial impurity was a double offense to the Jews.

After the death of Herod in 4 B.C., his territory was divided among his three sons. Archelaus was given Judea, Sa-

Dürer (German, 1471 – 1528), The Flight into Egypt
The Metropolitan Museum of Art, gift of Junius S. Morgan, 1919

maria and Idumea. He had none of his father's ability and spent ten years suppressing revolts with great cruelty. Finally the people whom he ruled appealed to Rome for help and Rome decided that instead of installing another king they would put a Roman official in charge of the area. Archelaus was banished and the first of the Roman procurators took over in A.D. 6. The procurator was responsible to the Emperor in Rome. His responsibility was keeping peace and supervising the part of the government which was the concern of Rome: the collection of taxes, the maintenance of garrisons, the construction of public buildings. The affairs of the people were left to local jurisdiction. This meant that in Jerusalem the Sanhedrin, or religious court presided over by the high priest, was the body which decided on local matters.

In the meantime the two brothers of Archelaus had better luck in ruling. Herod Antipas had been given the territory of Galilee and Perea, with the title of tetrarch, and Philip was given other territory to the north. Herod Antipas ruled until A.D. 39 when he fell into disfavor with the emperor and was banished.

During the adult life of Jesus, then, there were two different governments within the territory in which he lived. Galilee was under Herod Antipas as tetrarch, and Jerusalem was under procurators with local affairs handled by the Sanhedrin. Pontius Pilate was procurator when Jesus was crucified.

The Sects of Judaism

At the time of Jesus there were many sects or divisions of Judaism. These sects all came under the general heading of Judaism and shared many things in common, but in their practices and beliefs they differed from one another. Some of these sects are mentioned by name in the New Testament, and others underlie some of the thoughts expressed there. To understand them we must move back into history several centuries.

The Synagogue

During the Babylonian Exile which began in 586 B.C. following the destruction of Jerusalem by the Babylonians and the deportation of a large part of the population into exile in Babylon, many problems arose concerning the practice of religion. The people had thought that their one god could be worshipped in only one place, and that place was the house of God, the Temple of Jerusalem. There the sacrifices to him were made, and there all the celebrations were held. Devout followers of God had to go to Jerusalem to celebrate the holy days properly. They believed it could be done in no other place. Then disaster struck. The Holy City was destroyed and along with it the Temple.

The people asked, how could God be worshipped now that the Temple was gone? Jeremiah and Deutero-Isaiah (the name given to the 40th through the 55th chapters of the Book of Isaiah) who preached during this period insisted that God was not localized, but that he was where his people were. He could be worshipped in Babylon as well as in Jerusalem. Other leaders besides the prophets realized that if the Hebrew people were to hold together as a people, and if their religion was to survive, there must be means of practicing it. The result of this was the rise of the synagogue which became so important in New Testament times.

A synagogue was originally simply a place of meeting. Here the exiles would gather to hear one of their number read from the Law, to discuss their mutual problems and to worship. These synagogues were not meant to replace the

Temple in Jerusalem. They believed that there was only one Temple, and that it would have to be rebuilt as soon as possible. A continuation of this distinction is seen today in the different names which Jewish people call their places of worship. The Orthodox Jews call their places of worship synagogues because they believe that there can be only one Temple. The Reformed Jews, on the other hand, call their places of worship temples because they do not believe in the idea of there being only one Temple. They say that any place where worship is carried out is a temple.

Accompanying this synagogue development there was a slow and subtle change in practices which later became obvious and important. This change was in the way in which the Law was to be observed. It was one thing to be living in a small country with neighbors who all practiced the same religion. Under such circumstances it was quite easy to obey rules and regulations which covered many aspects of living. However, it was quite a different matter to be living in a strange city, surrounded by many people whose religion was dissimilar and whose customs were unlike. Life in the big, cosmopolitan city of Babylon was not like that of the little towns surrounding Jerusalem, nor even like that of Jerusalem itself. Therefore, the meetings in the synagogues devoted a good part of their time to what was known as the exposition of the Law. This simply means the interpretation of the law so that it would apply to the circumstances under which the Hebrews found themselves living. For example, the Law states how various rituals shall be carried out, but the Temple and a priest are assumed. How could these rituals be carried out in a strange land, and by whom? Substitutions had to be made and modifications allowed to permit the practice of the religion away from home. Since many of the daily activities of the Hebrews were ritualistic, eventually these interpretations grew to large proportions. The original Law was called the Torah (known in Greek as the Pentateuch), the five books of Moses which are the first five books in our

Old Testament. The commentary which sprang up on them is called the Mishnah, and the commentary on the Mishnah is called the Gemerah. The Mishnah and the Gemerah together are known as the Talmud. These were not gathered into an organized work until many centuries later. The Exile merely saw the start of the process of adapting the Law to fit various circumstances.

Later, after the Hebrews were allowed to return to their country and to rebuild their city and their Temple, the synagogue continued as an institution. There were places in Palestine which were remote enough to make attendance at the Temple in Jerusalem with any regularity an impossibility. All Jews, however, were supposed to visit the Temple at least once during their lifetime, and more often for the Holy Days if possible. Week in and week out they went to the synagogue where they could hear the Law expounded or a selection from the Prophets read. By the time of Jesus every little town had its synagogue which was the center of religious life for the community. It was there that the education of the boys in the town took place under the leadership of the rabbi, which means teacher. The synagogue was also the place where community problems were discussed, and so it was the center of political as well as religious activity.

The Pharisees

In connection with this synagogue development, there arose a group of men whose name is closely associated with it. These were the Pharisees. Exactly what the name means is not known, although it seems to mean "the separated ones." Separated from what we do not know for certain. Perhaps the separation was from uncleaness or "sin," perhaps it referred to that group who first supported Judas Maccabaeus and then separated from his successors as they became worldly and power seeking or maybe it meant simply that these were men who separated out one meaning of the Law from another. It does not really matter.

This sect accepted the additions to the Law made in the form of commentaries. They accepted some of the ideas which had come into Judaism, probably from the Persian religion with which Judaism had come in contact during the Exile. Such ideas were the belief in angels and the idea of life after death. The Pharisees also looked forward to the coming of a Messiah, or deliverer. They were intensely nationalistic and wanted to keep their religion and their nation free from any outside interference. The Maccabees and their followers were all Pharisees. The term scribe, which we often read in the Gospels, means simply one who could write, one who was a scholar. The scribes of the Pharisees would be the scholars who were Pharisees. These men were often the leaders of their group.

The Sadducees

The Sadducees, another group mentioned in the New Testament, were largely found in Jerusalem around the Temple. These men were closely connected with Temple worship. Their interest lay in seeing that it was continued and that it was kept pure. They were residents of the city. These factors combined to make the Sadducees more worldly than the Pharisees. They felt that if they could get along with the conqueror in ways which did not affect their religious worship, that this was the sensible thing to do. This group, therefore, accepted the Hellenization of their culture under the Greek rule. On the other hand, they would accept none of the oral Law, but maintained that the only true Law was that written in the Torah. They accepted none of the ideas not found there, such as the belief in the afterlife, angels or the coming of a Messiah. The Sadducees were mostly priests joined by some of the aristocracy of Jerusalem.

It seems something of a paradox that the Pharisees who accepted many ideas not found in the Torah should be the more conservative of the two groups, whereas the group known generally to be more liberal was the more narrow in what was accepted religiously. But this was the fact. The reason lies in the separation which the Sadducees made between their religious belief and their everyday life. The religion was kept pure and simple. It seemed not to matter whether in everyday life alien factors were introduced. If religious practice could be continued as it had always been, then compromise in other things was a small price to pay. The Pharisees, on the other hand, permeated their entire life with religious meaning. The Law had been interpreted to cover all phases of everyday life. Therefore to the Pharisees any attempt to change the daily living was an attack on religion itself. To understand this is to understand the actions of a Judas Maccabaeus. It is also to understand the criticisms made of Jesus and the criticisms which he made in regard to the observance of the Law.

The Essenes

Another sect which played an important role in the first century A.D. was the group known as the Essenes. The name seems to have meant "the pious ones," and it probably stems from the fact that the group practiced a strict observance of the Law. What the origin of the group was no one at the present time knows, but the Essenes had their roots in the same historical events as did the Pharisees and the Sadducees.

The Essenes did not take part in the Temple worship, because they did not believe in animal sacrifice nor in the rituals practiced there. In their stead, they placed great emphasis on ritual washings or baptism and on a sacred meal which was shared by the group. Their property was held in common so there was no individual wealth. There seem to have been followers of the Essenes who withdrew from the world into the desert, and there, separated from the rest of mankind, carried out the practice of religion as they felt it should be carried out. There seem also to have been adherents of the group who lived in the towns and villages. Some of the ancient historians mention the Essenes. Josephus, for example, tells us quite a bit about them, and so does Philo. It may be that the monastery at Qumran was an Essene monastery and that the Dead Sea Scrolls belonged to their library. At least if this group was not Essene it was a group closely related to them. The discoveries at Qumran are therefore of interest to us for what they can tell us about a group not mentioned in the New Testament, but contemporary with it.

Apocalyptic Writers

Another group which had a profound influence on New Testament thought and so eventually on Christianity, was not a sect with special religious practices, but a group of religious thinkers and writers known as the apocalyptic writers. Apocalyptic means a discovery or disclosure. Their writing was characterized by the wide use of symbols, especially animal symbols which stood for people and nations which were being described. These books were written during times of oppression to give hope to the oppressed. Because they were often full of venom against the ruler, they had to be veiled and obscure in meaning to protect the authors. For this reason they were written anonymously, and they pretended to be writing about something which happened centuries before. Those who read them could see their modern relevance, however.

Such a book is Revelation, written during the persecution of Domitian in A.D. 95. An early apocalypse is the Book of Daniel in the Old Testament which was written during the oppression of Antiochus Epiphanes. More important than the symbolism and the obscure writing, however, was the idea of the Messiah and the Kingdom of God which was put forth by this school of writers.

The Messiah and the Kingdom of God

Within Judaism, from the day of the Prophets on, there had been a hope that sometime in the future Israel would be raised up by God to take a foremost place in the world, ahead of all nations. The message of the Prophets had been that this would not happen until the nation as a whole had repented of her sins and had turned again to the obedience to God which was essential for this glory to occur. How this obedience should be carried out was a matter of debate. Some felt it was through strict attention to the Law and through careful observance of religious rituals. The Prophets thundered against this kind of externalism and legalism and stressed the need of leading an ethically pure life. Both groups looked forward to a time when their people would be part of an ideal kingdom which would be both peaceful and rich. The idea grew that there would rise up in the land a man like King David who had ruled hundreds of years before over a territory as large as any held since. He had brought peace to his people. This one "like David" was called the Messiah, and the ideal kingdom was called the Kingdom of God.

The apocalyptic writers introduced a new concept of Messiah and the Kingdom of God. Because of the long persecutions and the centuries of domination by alien powers, the idea of an earthly king who would bring the era of peace and plenty seemed impossible. To accomplish this task would require a supernatural being. This supernatural being, said the apocalyptic writer, would come at a future date on the clouds of glory. He would usher in a kingdom, not of this world, where all the enemies of the Jewish people would be crushed and the Israelites would enjoy a wonderful paradise free from all the worries and strife which they had been suffering. These ideas soon developed into theories of life after death. Since these things could not be accomplished on earth, nor in the lifetime of those living, there would be a future resurrection of those who had died; a Judgment Day to be followed by the ideal kingdom, a kingdom not of this world for this world would be destroyed.

The combination of these two ideas, that of the Davidic king ruling over an earthly Kingdom of God, and that of the apocalyptic Kingdom of God brought in by a Messiah coming on clouds of glory, can be seen in the Christian book of Revelation in which there is predicted a millenium (a thousand years) of earthly paradise, followed by the end of the world and the heavenly Kingdom for the righteous.

There seems to have been still another idea of the Messiah which is found reflected in the New Testament, but which is clearly set forth in the Dead Sea Scrolls. This idea was that a prophet, not a king, would arise in the land, a prophet like Moses who would be the deliverer.

In popular thought at the time of Jesus another Old Testament figure was important. Elijah was expected to live again and to appear on earth to announce the coming of the Messiah. His role was as a "forerunner." The Messiah himself was known by several names. Messiah means "anointed one" and is Hebrew. The Greek equivalent is "Christ" which also means "anointed one." In addition, the term "Son of

God" was used to designate the Messiah, and on occasion, the term "Son of Man" was also used. However, "Son of Man" was a term which sometimes meant "prophet" and sometimes just "man," i.e. a member of the human race.

All these ideas were current in the time of Jesus. Part of our difficulty in attempting to understand him is that the authors of the Gospels, believing that Jesus was the long awaited Messiah, attempted to make him fulfill all of these roles so that they could convince those to whom they were writing that he was, indeed, the Messiah. Sometimes these ideas are confusing and even contradictory as we have seen from our study of the birth stories. What did Jesus really think his role was? The ideas and interpretations of many people obscure our direct view of him.

Chapter Six: Paul

The Gospels, as we have seen, were written from 35 to 80 years after the death of Jesus. We have noted that the thinking of the early church influenced the writing of these Gospels and undoubtedly left its impress in the interpretation which was given to various events in the life of Jesus. Since Jesus was at the beginning of Christianity, and since the Gospels stand first in our New Testament, it is easy to fall into the habit of thinking that they were the earliest pieces of writing in the New Testament. This is not the case. The Epistles of Paul were written earlier. To understand the Gospels fully, and thereby gain a keener understanding of the thoughts of Jesus himself, one really needs to know about that remarkable early Christian who so skillfully directed the thinking of this movement that his influence is still strongly apparent today. How can we learn about him?

There are two places in the New Testament where we can glean some facts about Paul. First of all there are the Pauline Epistles, letters which were written by Paul himself: Romans, Corinthians, Galatians, Philippians, Colossians, Thessalonians, Philemon. The other Epistles in the New Testament were written later, although some of them have been credited to Paul.

Second there is the Book of Acts which, as we have seen, is the second volume of the work of Luke. Acts tells the story of the spread of Christianity throughout the eastern Mediterranean world from just after the death of Jesus to the time when Paul went to Rome.

Of the two sources, the Epistles are the earlier, having been written by Paul between A.D. 50 and 60 to churches which he had earlier visited and to which he continued to give help by letter. Acts was, of course, written some 30 or 40 years later. We are fortunate to have some of the actual letters of Paul. There are also some sermons in Acts which are supposed to be his, but they may well have been altered with the passage of time. For the events in Paul's life we must rely on the few glimpses we are given in the letters and in the book of Acts. Whether all the details are correct is doubtful. However, the story of his life as it is recorded in the New Testament has been accepted for centuries. In broad outline we can continue to accept it until some proof is offered that it is incorrect.

Paul's Life

Paul was named Saul by his family. Apparently he took the name of Paul after his conversion to Christianity. Saul is the Jewish form of the name and Paul (or Paulus) is the Roman. He was born and brought up in the seacoast town of Tarsus in Asia Minor, where he was probably given the typical Jewish education of his time. He learned to read and write Hebrew in the synagogue school, and in addition he was taught a trade as were all boys, even though they might, as did Paul, want to pursue the profession of teacher and scholar. Paul learned the trade of tent making which may have included the making of sails as well. When he was a young man he went to Jerusalem where he is supposed to have studied with a famous rabbi of the time named Gamaliel. Gamaliel was a Pharisee, and apparently Paul studied with him in order that he, too, might become a Pharisaic rabbi.

Here Paul developed a deep hatred of the Christians whom he considered heretics. The story is told in Acts of Paul holding the coats of the men who were assigned to stone Stephen, one of the early Christians who became the religion's first martyr. Stoning was a method of executing people which preceded the firing squad and is based on the same principle. Since each person in a group throws a stone, no one of them feels solely responsible for the victim's death. As a rabbinical student Paul could not actually take part in the stoning because he would then have blood on his hands and, therefore, be unclean. It was all right for him to hold the coats of those who did the job, however. This kind of fine, legalistic distinction between what was right and what was not was one of the things about the Pharisees which Paul criticized in later years.

The stoning of Stephen seems to have made a deep impression on Paul. The serenity with which this Christian faced death was unnerving to him. At this point there apparently stirred in him a deep discontent which for the moment simply spurred him to more frantic action in persecuting the Christians.

Soon after the stoning, Luke tells in Acts, Paul journeyed to the city of Damascus where he was pursuing the leaders of the Christian movement who had fled there to escape the persecution. On the road to Damascus, Paul had a vision in which Jesus appeared to him and said, "Saul, Saul why do you persecute me?" Paul fell down in a trance in the dust on the road and when he arose he was blind! On his arrival in Damascus one of the Christians instructed by a vision from God, so says the book of Acts, found him and healed him miraculously of his blindness.

Paul was thereupon baptized and became a Christian. At first he had understandable difficulty in being accepted by the Christians. They felt that he was probably tricking them in order to persecute them further. They did finally accept him, but then he had difficulty with the Jews who were furious with him for having become a Christian. The story is told in Acts of how the Christians let him down over the city wall in Damascus in a basket because all the gates were being watched by the Jews, and they feared for his life if he tried to escape by ordinary means.

The traditional date of Paul's conversion is A.D. 34. We may question whether his conversion was so sudden as it seems to have been. Time has probably erased the intervening details of the story and telescoped the highlights into one great drama. It is a fact, however, that Saul the Pharisee became Paul the Christian missionary. What he did in the years immediately after his conversion or where he went is obscure. It is apparent that he spent the time preparing himself for his new work and keeping out of sight until the wrath of the Jews should have passed and the Christian group be fully ready to accept him as one of their number. After this interval of six or seven years, Paul began to preach.

Traditionally, he is supposed to have made three missionary journeys, and a final, fourth journey to Rome. The itinerary of these journeys is found by reading Acts. There is grave doubt that the details of these journeys are accurate, due to the passage of time between them and the telling about them. There are events and places mentioned in the letters which are not in Acts, giving an indication of other cities visited and other journeys made which are not included there. We do know the sequence of events, however, and regardless of how many cities may have been visited we also know this spreader of the Gospel traveled a tremendous number of miles and preached to a large number of people. He had an enthusiasm and a zeal which won many converts to the new religion. It was he who planted the seeds of Christianity all over Asia Minor, Greece, Cyprus and perhaps even Rome itself. And all this traveling was done by boat or on foot or donkey! To what extent the actual survival of Christianity may be attributed to him we will never know, but that Paul contributed greatly to its ability to continue in the face of dreadful persecution and opposition is above question.

Paul died a prisoner in Rome where he had been held for nearly ten years. He was arrested in Jerusalem during a riot on the steps of the Temple and appealed to the Roman emperor for justice as was his right as a Roman citizen. He did not want to go on trial before the Sanhedrin, for he knew that there he would not have a chance. Tradition tells us that he was killed during the persecutions of Nero in A.D. 64 along with Peter.

The Importance of Paul

Why is it that Paul is so important in the study of early Christianity? To understand his thinking is difficult. The details of his life are obscure. In many ways his character was not pleasant: he had a low opinion of women, he was fanatic in his espousal of Christianity, he placed little value on the ability of mankind and he seems to have been unattractive physically as well. Yet he shaped Christianity for all centuries to come. One of the reasons for this was undoubtedly his ability to systematize the doctrines of Christianity in a way which made them straightforward and easy for people to understand and so to accept.

Some believe that in doing this he twisted the teaching of Jesus into something which Jesus had never meant it to be. Certainly the religion of Paul is a religion *about* Jesus rather than the religion *of* Jesus, but it was that almost as soon as Jesus was dead. If it had not been changed in this way it would have been a form of Judaism and not Christianity at all, for Jesus was a Jew. An element in the early spread of Christianity which is often overlooked is that Paul was not the only missionary preaching during the first century. There were many others. The names of some of them are mentioned in the Book of Acts and in the Epistles. It is unfortunate that the final rite which insured salvation for him. These rites were often crude and barbaric, but to the miserable, the slaves, the poor, the men without hope, they gave promise of a better day to come. Associated with each of these mysteries was a figure like a god who died and rose again, just as nature dies and rises again in the spring. In various ways, by participating in this rebirth, the initiates achieved their desire, the promise of eternal life. There is much in the language of Paul which reflects this language of the mystery religions.

Paul really lived in two worlds. He was brought up in the Greek world of paganism, but as a Jew. He had a thorough education in the Judaism of his day and he understood it well. He found that the Judaism of the Pharisees did not satisfy his inner longings. Its endless legalisms did not spell salvation for him. There were too many ways in which he could fall short and fail to live up to the demands of the Law. He felt he could never work his way out of the morass, and ... made pagan or mystery religion unap... ... came in contact with ...

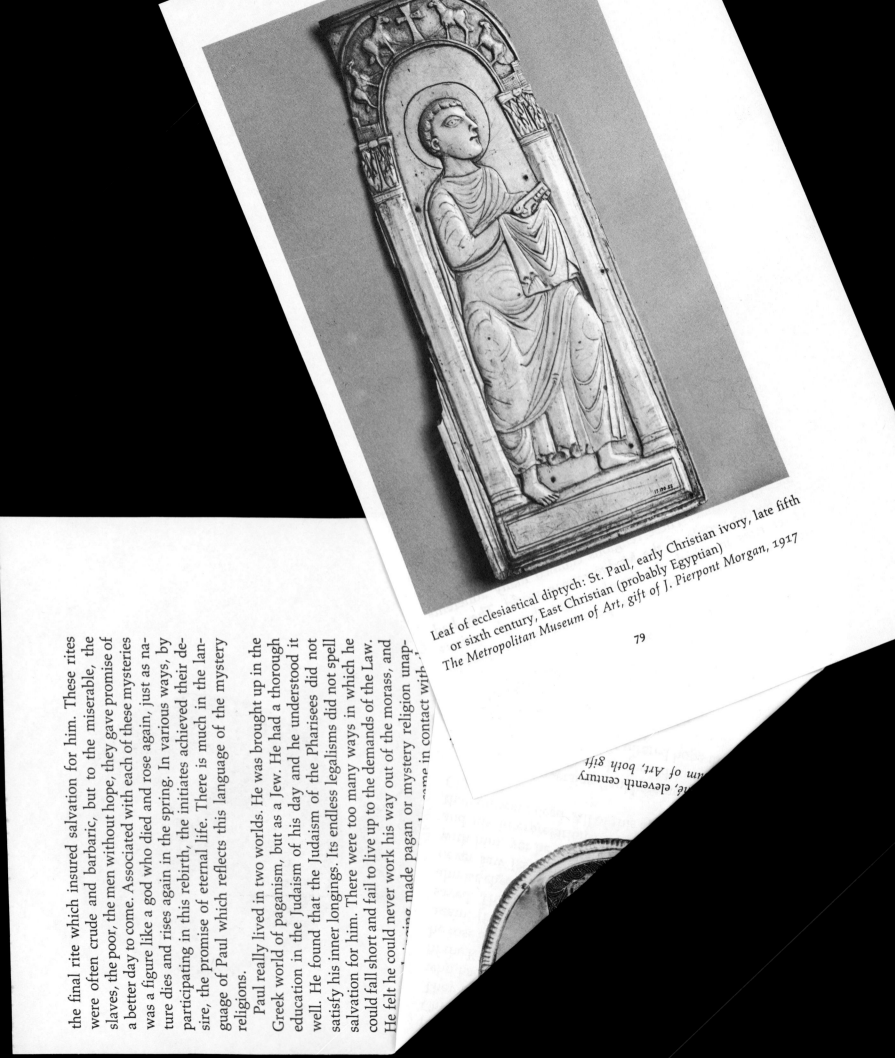

Leaf of ecclesiastical diptych: St. Paul, early Christian ivory, late fifth or sixth century, East Christian (probably Egyptian)
The Metropolitan Museum of Art, gift of J. Pierpont Morgan, 1917

79

we have no account of their teaching and their journeys to compare with Paul's. Many of them undoubtedly had as great an impact on the groups to whom they talked, and their message may have been different from his. Yet it was the letters Paul wrote which survived, and it was about Paul that Luke wrote in Acts. If some of the writings and deeds of the other missionaries had survived, how different would Christianity be today? It is an interesting question, which we cannot answer.

What Did Paul Teach?

It has often been stated that in Paul the Jesus of history became the Christ of faith. In a sense this is true. In reading the letters of Paul one searches in vain for any clue to the personality of Jesus. There is little reference to statements made by Jesus, and in fact no reference at all to Jesus as a man, a human being who lived and breathed and taught. And yet these same letters are permeated with the spirit which was in Jesus. Paul's advice to the people of Corinth, expressed in I and II Corinthians, is advice given with the same feeling of compassion, and with the same disdain of the trivial or the unimportant which we associate with Jesus. Paul's main emphasis is, however, on the cross and on the belief in the resurrection with its implications for the believer.

To understand this, one must remember who P...
was a man well acquainted with the Hell...
he must have known much abo...
ously knew about the...
ular in his time...
among...

(a) St. Paul
(b) Christ
Byzantine enamels cloison...
The Metropolitan Muse...
1917

Leaf of ecclesiastical diptych: St. Paul, early Christian ivory, late fifth
   or sixth century, East Christian (probably Egyptian)
The Metropolitan Museum of Art, gift of J. Pierpont Morgan, 1917

we have no account of their teaching and their journeys to compare with Paul's. Many of them undoubtedly had as great an impact on the groups to whom they talked, and their message may have been different from his. Yet it was the letters Paul wrote which survived, and it was about Paul that Luke wrote in Acts. If some of the writings and deeds of the other missionaries had survived, how different would Christianity be today? It is an interesting question, which we cannot answer.

What Did Paul Teach?

It has often been stated that in Paul the Jesus of history became the Christ of faith. In a sense this is true. In reading the letters of Paul one searches in vain for any clue to the personality of Jesus. There is little reference to statements made by Jesus, and in fact no reference at all to Jesus as a man, a human being who lived and breathed and taught. And yet these same letters are permeated with the spirit which was in Jesus. Paul's advice to the people of Corinth, expressed in I and II Corinthians, is advice given with the same feeling of compassion, and with the same disdain of the trivial or the unimportant which we associate with Jesus. Paul's main emphasis is, however, on the cross and on the belief in the resurrection with its implications for the believer.

To understand this, one must remember who Paul was. He was a man well acquainted with the Hellenistic world so that he must have known much about pagan worship. He obviously knew about the mystery religions which were so popular in his time. These religions claimed many adherents among the people of the Mediterranean world. They had secret rites in which the member went through various stages of initiation until he was permitted to participate in the final rite which insured salvation for him. These rites were often crude and barbaric, but to the miserable, the slaves, the poor, the men without hope, they gave promise of a better day to come. Associated with each of these mysteries was a figure like a god who died and rose again, just as nature dies and rises again in the spring. In various ways, by participating in this rebirth, the initiates achieved their desire, the promise of eternal life. There is much in the language of Paul which reflects this language of the mystery religions.

Paul really lived in two worlds. He was brought up in the Greek world of paganism, but as a Jew. He had a thorough education in the Judaism of his day and he understood it well. He found that the Judaism of the Pharisees did not satisfy his inner longings. Its endless legalisms did not spell salvation for him. There were too many ways in which he could fall short and fail to live up to the demands of the Law. He felt he could never work his way out of the morass, and yet his upbringing made pagan or mystery religion unappealing to him. It was then that he came in contact with the Christians. They were sure and happy in their simple faith. They believed that God had sent his son, Jesus the Messiah, who had lived among them and preached about the coming of the Kingdom of God. He was crucified but on the third day he rose again, thus proving that it was possible for all to rise again. If we believe this, the Christians taught, we will be saved. This faith enabled such a man as Stephen to endure almost cheerfully the most dreadful death. Paul apparently never saw Jesus in person, although he was contemporary with him, yet he undoubtedly knew of his ethical teaching and his interpretation of religion as inner attitude rather than outward deed. All of this appealed to him. He became a Christian.

After his conversion Paul became a devoted Christian. He felt that the whole world should know the beauty of this faith of his. It was true. It offered hope to a suffering world.

(a) St. Paul
(b) Christ
Byzantine enamels *cloisonné*, eleventh century
The Metropolitan Museum of Art, both gift of J. Pierpont Morgan,
  1917

Everyone should accept it. In attempting to make this faith comprehensible to the Greek world, a world he knew so well, he translated many of the terms and concepts into language which they would understand. He borrowed words from the mystery religions to explain what he meant to the followers of those religions. He took ideas from the Greek philosophers to attempt to make comprehensible his conception of Christ. He used the word Christ or "anointed one" rather than the Jewish word Messiah when he was speaking to the Greek world.

But to say that Paul transformed the Jesus of history into the Christ of faith is to oversimplify what happened. The Disciples were really the ones who transformed Jesus. It was they who believed in the resurrection, who labeled Jesus as the Messiah and who looked for his return to earth again. Paul was converted to this religion of the Disciples. He transformed their simple faith into terms comprehensible to the Greek-speaking world. He put system into it. He articulated its basic concepts, but he remain true also to the ethical spirit of Jesus.

What actually did Paul believe? This is a difficult question and one which has puzzled theologians for centuries. Paul had a brilliant mind. Since he was thinking as he went along, we do not always find consistent views in his letters. No one thinks exactly the same throughout his whole life. Just as our ideas change, so did Paul's. We cannot see the evolution of his thinking because we cannot date his letters precisely enough. Therefore, we cannot be sure of their order. Also since he wrote to different churches in different places with different problems, his letters were written in a way which would be understandable and helpful to a particular situation. This led to inconsistencies, too. However, some basic ideas do stand out.

Paul believed that the nature of man is basically and hopelessly evil. Man can try to lead the good life, to do those things which he knows he should do, but he will find this a hopeless task. One part of him knows better, so to speak, but the other part keeps dragging him back. There is, therefore, a necessity for help. This help can come only from God, but man is separated from God because of his sinful nature. There is need for God and man to become reconciled. This reconciliation is brought about by faith in God's son who was sent to earth in the body of a man, Jesus. The crucifixion was the sacrifice which God's son made to enable all mankind to be reconciled to God once again. The resurrection is the promise that this reconciliation is possible. Through faith in Christ man is not only reconciled to God, he really deserves to be accepted by God. "Justified by faith" is the term which Paul uses.

One accepts this faith through the rite of baptism in which one becomes dead to the evil self and is born again into the new. From that time onward all the old ways of religion can be left behind and the deep faith one has in Christ crucified and resurrected is all one needs. However, Paul sets forth a stiff demand on the new Christians as far as behavior is concerned. To show that one is truly a Christian it is necessary to hold to a high moral standard. Just because one is free from the shackles of the old religious laws and rules does not mean that a person can do just what he wants to do. Far from it. The standard which he must maintain is higher than that which he had before. If he fails to maintain it, it shows that he does not have faith and the love for God which he pretends he has.

There is a great deal more which could be said about Paul. His was a fascinating life. It is important that we understand him to the best of our ability, for it is through his teaching that Christianity grew. His imprint is also on the Gospels. What he believed and taught is reflected there, and as we turn to them we should be watching for signs of his interpretation as we attempt to get behind the times and thought of Paul to the figure of Jesus himself.

Chapter Seven: Jesus

The Birth

At the beginning of this book we began a search for the facts about the birth of Jesus. We found that we did not have information enough to answer the questions which we had posed for ourselves. Now that we have explored some of the background of the New Testament we can turn again to the start which we made and attempt to answer those questions.

Take out the notes which you made on this material. Go back over the questions you asked at the beginning and try to answer them again. See if you have different reasons now for thinking why each event was reported by the Gospel writer. Why did Matthew include things which Luke left out? Why did Luke include things which Matthew left out?

We did not read all of the first part of Luke, so this is a good time to finish it. There you will find the story of Elizabeth, the mother of John the Baptist, and her husband Zechariah who was so amazed that they were going to have a baby that he was struck dumb until after the baby actually arrived. There, too, are some lovely poems which scholars think may have been added to the Gospels at a later date. They are probably some of the earliest Christian hymns.

We are ready now to ask when Jesus was born. This is not an easy question to answer. If we list all the historical figures mentioned by any of the Gospels in connection with the birth of Jesus, we find that according to Matthew, Jesus was born toward the end of the reign of Herod the King, since Herod died while the family was in Egypt (Matthew 2: 1 and 19). Luke tells us that it was a decree of Caesar Augustus when Quirinius was governor of Syria that sent Joseph and Mary to Bethlehem (Luke 2:2). Augustus was Emperor from 27 B.C. to A.D. 14. There was a census under Quirinius in A.D. 6 but Herod died in 4 B.C! Some scholars think that Luke was confused as to which census was ordered at the time of Jesus' birth and meant one in 6 B.C. Others think that the census was not an actual one, but that it was used by Luke as a probable reason for Joseph and Mary to go to Bethlehem. If we accept Matthew's statement that Jesus was born before Herod died, then he would have to be born at the latest in 4 B.C., and if the census is also to be taken into account, the date would have to be 6 B.C. There is no information at all on the month, or the day of the month, in which he was born. The date of December 25th was set as the day to celebrate his birth probably sometime in the second century.

When we have completed our study, what do we know about the birth of Jesus? We know he was born, and that is all we are sure about. The exact circumstances will probably forever remain a mystery. Why, then, do we celebrate Christmas as his birthday? And why do we repeat all the stories from Matthew and Luke which are obviously more in the realm of myth than history? These two Gospel writers tried to answer the questions which people were asking about the origin of Jesus in the only way they could. It was as though they said, "This is what the man was like, and so these things must have happened." This does not mean that they were insincere or hypocritical or deceitful. Quite the contrary. They had such an overwhelming admiration and love for Jesus that their books about his life breathe their feelings on every page. Can you think of examples of myths about famous men of our era?

Christmas was a holiday which had been celebrated for centuries before Jesus. If we discovered that Jesus was born on August 15, when and how do you think we would celebrate Christmas? We should forget our literal-mindedness when we read these accounts and enjoy them for what they are: beautiful, poetic tributes to a life which was greatly admired. In the words of the carol:

> O hush the noise, ye men of strife,
> and hear the angels sing!

The Visit to the Temple

According to Luke, Jesus was "about thirty years of age" when he began his ministry (Luke 3:23). Strange as it may seem, there is only one Gospel story about his childhood, youth and early adulthood. The one exception is the story of the visit to the Temple which is told in Luke 2:41-51. Just ten verses to cover the events of thirty years! Some scholars have even doubted the authenticity of this. Others have maintained that the story has the ring of truth because Jesus and his parents seem so human and alive in it. If it had not happened, what would have been the reason for including it? Read it, and see what you think. Here are some questions you might ask yourself.

Do you think it possible for a twelve-year-old boy to amaze a group of learned teachers with his "understanding and his answers" (Luke 2: 47)?

What do you think of Mary's reaction when she discovered Jesus was missing (Luke 2: 48)?

What do you think Jesus meant by his reply to her (Luke 2:49)?

For what reason do you think Luke might have included the story even if he had no assurance that it was true?

The Baptism

The first event in Jesus' life which is included in all four Gospels is his baptism in the River Jordan by John the Baptist. Following are the accounts from the three Synoptic Gospels. We are not including John in this study for the reasons which we discussed in Chapter Three.

Mark 1:1-11
The beginning of the gospel of Jesus Christ, the Son of God. 2 As it is written in Isaiah the prophet,
"Behold, I send my messenger before thy face,
who shall prepare thy way;
[3] the voice of one crying in the wilderness:
Prepare the way of the Lord, make his paths straight—"
[4] John the baptizer appeared in the wilderness, preaching a baptism of repentance for the forgiveness of sins. [5] And there went out to him all the country of Judea, and all the people of Jerusalem; and they were baptized by him in the river Jordan, confessing their sins. [6] Now John was clothed with camel's hair, and had a leather girdle around his waist, and ate locusts and wild honey. [7] And he preached, saying, "After me comes he who is mightier than I, the thong of whose sandals I am not worthy to stoop down and untie. [8] I have baptized you with water; but he will baptize you with the Holy Spirit."
9 In those days Jesus came from Nazareth of Galilee and was baptized by John in the Jordan. [10] And when he came up out of the water, immediately he saw the heavens opened and the Spirit descending upon him like a dove; [11] and a voice came from heaven, "Thou art my beloved Son; with thee I am well pleased."

Matthew 3:1-17
In those days came John the Baptist, preaching in the wilderness of Judea, [2] "Repent, for the kingdom of heaven is at hand." [3] For this is he who was spoken of by the prophet Isaiah when he said,
"The voice of one crying in the wilderness:
Prepare the way of the Lord, make his paths straight."
[4] Now John wore a garment of camel's hair, and a leather girdle around his waist; and his food was locusts and wild honey. [5] Then went out to him Jerusalem and all Judea and all the region about the Jordan, [6] and they were baptized by him in the river Jordan, confessing their sins.
7 But when he saw many of the Pharisees and Sad'ducees coming for baptism, he said to them, "You brood of vipers! Who warned you to flee from the wrath to come? [8] Bear fruit that befits repentance, [9] and do not presume to say to yourselves, 'We have Abraham as our father'; for I tell you, God is able from these stones to raise up chil-

dren to Abraham. [10] Even now the axe is laid to the root of the trees; every tree therefore that does not bear good fruit is cut down and thrown into the fire.

[11] "I baptize you with water for repentance, but he who is coming after me is mightier than I, whose sandals I am not worthy to carry; he will baptize you with the Holy Spirit and with fire. [12] His winnowing fork is in his hand, and he will clear his threshing floor and gather his wheat into the granary, but the chaff he will burn with unquenchable fire."

[13] Then Jesus came from Galilee to the Jordan to John, to be baptized by him. [14] John would have prevented him, saying, "I need to be baptized by you, and do you come to me?" [15] But Jesus answered him, "Let it be so now; for thus it is fitting for us to fulfill all righteousness." Then he consented. [16] And when Jesus was baptized, he went up immediately from the water, and behold, the heavens were opened and he saw the Spirit of God descending like a dove, and alighting on him; [17] and lo, a voice from heaven saying, "This is my beloved Son, with whom I am well pleased."

Luke 3:1-17, 21-22

In the fifteenth year of the reign of Tibe'ri-us Caesar, Pontius Pilate being governor of Judea, and Herod being tetrarch of Galilee, and his brother Philip tetrarch of the region of Iturae'a and Trachoni'tis, and Lysa'ni-as tetrarch of Abile'ne, [2] in the high-priesthood of Annas and Ca'iaphas, the word of God came to John the son of Zechari'ah in the wilderness; [3] and he went into all the region about the Jordan, preaching a baptism of repentance for the forgiveness of sins. [4] As it is written in the book of the words of Isaiah the prophet,

"The voice of one crying in the wilderness:
Prepare the way of the Lord, make his paths straight.
[5] Every valley shall be filled,
and every mountain and hill shall be brought low,
and the crooked shall be made straight,
and the rough ways shall be made smooth;
[6] and all flesh shall see the salvation of God."

[7] He said therefore to the multitudes that came out to be baptized by him, "You brood of vipers! Who warned you to flee from the wrath to come? [8] Bear fruits that befit repentance, and do not begin to say to yourselves, 'We have Abraham as our father'; for I tell you, God is able from these stones to raise up children to Abraham. [9] Even now the axe is laid to the root of the tree; every tree therefore that does not bear good fruit is cut down and thrown into the fire."

10 And the multitudes asked him, "What then shall we do?" [11] And he answered them, "He who has two coats, let him share with him who has none; and he who has food, let him do likewise." [12] Tax collectors also came to be baptized, and said to him, "Teacher, what shall we do?" [13] And he said to them, "Collect no more than is appointed you." [14] Soldiers also asked him, "And we, what shall we do?" And he said to them, "Rob no one by violence or by false accusation, and be content with your wages."

15 As the people were in expectation, and all men questioned in their hearts concerning John, whether perhaps he were the Christ, [16] John answered them all, "I baptize you with water; but he who is mightier than I is coming, the thong of whose sandals I am not worthy to untie; he will baptize you with the Holy Spirit and with fire. [17] His winnowing fork is in his hand, to clear his threshing floor, and to gather the wheat into his granary, but the chaff he will burn with unquenchable fire."

21 Now when all the people were baptized, and when Jesus also had been baptized and was praying, the heaven was opened, [22] and the Holy Spirit descended upon him in bodily form, as a dove, and a voice came from heaven, "Thou art my beloved Son; with thee I am well pleased."

First let us look at the passages which are peculiar to each Gospel. Mark is the shortest. Note that all of Mark's account is included in the other two Gospels. Make a list of what each of the others adds.

> What does Matthew add to the Markan version which Luke does not?
>
> Why do you think he added this material?
>
> What did Luke add to the Markan version which Matthew did not?
>
> What reasons might Luke have had for adding this?

At first it would seem that Luke had given us some help in dating the events in the life of Jesus by telling us that the baptism occurred "in the fifteenth year of the reign of Tiberius Caesar." However, since Tiberius was co-regent before he was emperor and Luke does not tell us which he means, we have a choice of four years A.D. 26-30. He also

Rouault (French, 1871 – 1958), The Baptism. Aquatint, undated.
Courtesy of New York Public Library, Prints Division

does not tell us how long John had been baptizing before he baptized Jesus.

Compare the sermons of John the Baptist as reported by each Gospel writer.

Can you put them together and say what the essence of John's preaching was?

Compare the three versions of the baptism of Jesus.

What do you think happened?

After you try to answer this read the next paragraph which has some ideas which may help you to answer the question; or may change the answer you have given.

Do you think that this was a real happening? Real in the sense of being literally true? Have you ever tried to tell someone about a vivid dream you have had? Do you always say, "it seemed as though" or "in my dream"? Don't you frequently say, "I had a dream! I was running down the street in my bare feet when a huge wildcat jumped down from the top of a tree. . ."? What would happen if the sixth person after you failed to preface this story with the, "I had a dream"?

Or perhaps you have tried to tell someone what a deep feeling you have had is like, for example: what it is like to be "madly in love" or "boiling mad" or what it feels like to have something strike you as "terribly funny." Does thinking about these things help you understand the verses?

We can see the process of a story of an experience becoming more and more literal if we look at the part concerning the Holy Spirit. Look first in Mark 1:10, then in Matthew 3:16 and then Luke 3:22. What has happened to the simple Markan description of the Holy Spirit descending "like a dove"? Do you see how much more "real" that dove has become?

What do *you* think the experience of the baptism meant to Jesus?

John the Baptist

Jesus was baptized by a man named John the Baptist, who

"appeared in the wilderness" (Mark 1:4) "clothed in camel's hair" with "a leather girdle around his waist and ate locusts and wild honey" (Mark 1:6). Who was this strange man?

Luke tells us in the first chapter of his Gospel about John's miraculous birth, and of how Mary, the mother of Jesus, and Elizabeth, John's mother, were related. John's father, according to Luke, was priest of the Temple. The last verse in the chapter states simply, "And the child grew and became strong in spirit, and he was in the wilderness till the day of his manifestation to Israel" (Luke 1:80). From our previous reading of parts of the first chapter of Luke, we know that much of it is poetry. If this is true of the parts concerning Jesus, it will also be true of those concerning John. It is possible, of course, that John was of a priestly family and that he was related to Jesus, but there is no mention of this anywhere else in the New Testament. It seems more likely that these were surmises made at a later date as the early Christians began to wonder about the real connection between John and Jesus, and to ask questions about John's origin. Scholars today are studying these passages in an attempt to see if there may be a hint in them clothed in myth, of who John was and from where he came.

> For example, what does Luke mean "he was in the wilderness"?
> Was his home there?
> Was he an Essene living in such a place as Qumran?
> Or do you think this is a figure of speech?

We are not sure of anything about the early life of John. He just appears "out of the wilderness" as did the prophets of the Old Testament. His message of repentance sounds like the Old Testament prophets, too. The sight of a man coming out of the wilderness, dressed in skins, and thundering a message of "repent" would not be as strange to those of the first century as it would seem to us today. We would probably think such a person "crazy" and would not take him seriously. The people of John's day, on the other hand, would look on him as sent from God, and would believe that God literally spoke through him. He would be treated with great respect for this reason.

There are some other bits of information about John besides this preliminary appearance. The most dramatic of these concerns his death. Read about this in Mark 6: 14-29. Notice the respect King Herod seems to have had for John (Mark 6:16, 20, 26).

> Why do you think Herod thought that Jesus was John the Baptist come to life again (Mark 6:14-16)?
> Why was Herodias so angry at John (Mark 6:17-19)?
> From this story, what kind of a person do you think Salome, the daughter of Herodias, was?
> What do you think of Herod's action?

Write an account of this birthday party as though you were there. Include how you think you would have felt. Note that John had disciples (Mark 6:29).

John's disciples are also mentioned in Mark 2:18. Read the whole section Mark 2:18-22. What were John's disciples doing that the disciples of Jesus were not? Jesus' answer to those who questioned him is really three answers, perhaps given at three different times to the same or a similar question. See if you can explain each of these answers in your own words.

Another example of the esteem in which John the Baptist was held is seen in Mark 11:27-33. This passage also gives us a glimpse of Jesus in a difficult situation.

> What do you think of the answer which Jesus gave to his critics?
> What did people think of John?

In Matthew 11:2-15 we see again the importance of John. This passage is a little difficult to interpret, but it is clear that Jesus thought of John as a prophet and as an important prophet. The passage, written long after the fact, shows that Jesus was recognized by John as the Messiah, and that Jesus was thinking of John as Elijah, the prophet who would come to earth again to herald the Messiah. This is, of course, the traditional role of John as set forth in the story of the baptism (Mark 1:7-8; Matthew 3:11; Luke 3:16).

There is still another passage which gives a glimpse of John. This passage is Luke 11:1-4. Who is the author of this prayer? In Matthew it appears in a slightly different form and in a different setting as part of the Sermon on the Mount (Matthew 6:7-14). From this we would conclude that it is one of the teachings handed down by word of mouth which came from Jesus; this is why it is called the *Lord's* prayer, of course. However, it is possible that it may be an even older prayer which Jesus, and John before him, liked and used. The Lukan passage shows that John taught his disciples prayers, and so did Jesus. You might like to compare the two versions of the prayer.

Which appears to be the older?

Which do you like better?

In the Gospel of John, John the Baptist appears in a slightly different light from that in the Synoptics, and it seems almost as if the Gospel writer had attempted to make sure that no one thought John was important except to prepare the way for Jesus. Look at John 1:6-8, 15, 19-31.

This Gospel also tells us that some of John's disciples turned from him and followed Jesus (John 1:35-37). There seems to have been rivalry between these two groups, the followers of Jesus and the followers of John. We have seen this reflected in the section we just read in Luke about the prayer (see further: John 3:22-30; 4:1-3; 5:36; Acts 18: 24-25; 19:1-7). Thus it would seem that perhaps the followers of John did not accept his role as the forerunner of Jesus as quickly or as completely as one would suppose from quick reading of the Synoptics.

The whole mystery of the figure of John the Baptist is one which interests scholars at present. It seems obvious that John was a much greater figure in his time than we are led to suppose by the Gospels. This is understandable when we consider that the Gospels were written by followers of Jesus to prove that Jesus was the Messiah, and that everyone must become his follower. Yet there seems to have been a close connection between John and Jesus. Or do you think this close connection might have been exaggerated in order to appease the followers of John and to win them over to be followers of Jesus after John's death?

One answer has been suggested although it cannot be proven at the present time, and is still only a guess. The solution is this: John was an Essene who grew up "in the wilderness" at one of the desert centers of the Essenes. He disagreed with the Essene group and decided to go out to preach his essentially Old Testament message of repentance on his own. Jesus, too, was acquainted with the teachings of the Essenes, whether he ever belonged to the group or not, but his interpretation of the teaching was such that he could not be considered one of them. Thus, John and Jesus could be considered spiritual "cousins" in that their backgrounds were similar. After the death of both, their followers were preaching quite similar ideas, so that eventually the two groups merged. The Gospels, however, were written by the followers of Jesus. Therefore in them we have a distorted picture of John, in which John is made less important than he really was. These are all speculations, and as more research is done by Biblical scholars in this area, more speculation will be in order. The stature of John the Baptist is growing as we understand more about him.

In the light of what you now know, how would you state the role of John the Baptist? What do you think was his relation to Jesus?

The Temptation

The story of the temptation of Jesus is told in its simplest form in the Gospel of Mark. The more elaborate story, which

96

is more familiar through its illustration in art and sermons, is the version found in Matthew and Luke. The only major difference between these two Gospels is the reversal of the last two temptations.

Read Mark 1:12-13. What do you think Mark means by, "The Spirit immediately drove him out into the wilderness"?

Recall the baptism experience and your interpretation of it. Consider this in explaining the temptation experience.

What do you think "tempted by Satan" means? Try to put these two verses into your own words, so that a person who did not have any idea what Spirit, Satan or angels meant would understand.

Now read Matthew 4:1-11 and Luke 4:1-13. These two versions add three actual temptations to the simple account of Mark. Much has been written in the attempt to interpret these, but there is no single interpretation which is universally accepted, although almost all scholars today agree that the temptations are not actual events, but rather graphic descriptions of inner thoughts.

Since Matthew and Luke are almost identical in their telling of the temptation, let us use the Matthean version, and try to understand why these verses are so difficult to explain.

In this passage the Tempter says, "*If* you are the Son of God," then do these things (Matthew 4:3, 6). Jesus refused to do them. All three temptations represent popular ideas of great deeds which a Messiah could do. The first involves a miracle (Matthew 4:3). The second involves magic, not for a constructive end, but to prove the possession of supernatural power (Matthew 4:5-6). The third promises Jesus he will rule over all the world (Matthew 4:8-9), which would involve a compromise with evil.

The problem in interpretation is this: does this passage mean that Jesus was the Son of God, the Messiah, but not in the popular sense? In other words, does this passage mean that he was rejecting the idea of Messiah (that is, a wonder worker who would miraculously appear and rule the world), as it was commonly held? Was he putting another idea in its place? This is not explained in this passage, but it was obvious by the time the Gospel was written that Jesus did not do any of the things which are represented by the temptations. The passage could, then, be a story of the rejection of demands which Jesus knew would be made of him if he claimed to be Messiah. He rejected these ideas as unworthy of the Messiah. On the other hand, it is possible to interpret these passages to mean that Jesus answered the Tempter's, "*If* you are the Son of God" with a refusal to consider these challenges because he was really implying that he was *not* the Messiah. Read these passages again and see if you think that there are these two possible interpretations. Which would you choose?

There is still another possible point of view which avoids the problem of interpreting the temptations as actual thoughts of Jesus by considering them as insertions coming from writers of the Christian church at a later date in order to show that from the very beginning Jesus had rejected the popularly held ideas of Messiah. Such a theory would assume that the longer versions of Matthew and Luke were intended to answer the charge that Jesus could not be the Messiah since he did not fulfill these expectations.

Whatever our interpretation, it is clear that from the beginning Jesus did not think of himself as a ruler. This idea was not part of his concept of himself. The popular messianic hope was not to be fulfilled by him.

The Beginning of the Ministry

We are ready now to learn about those years in which Jesus preached and taught and during which he made such a profound impression on those who heard him that some

2000 years later we are trying to learn as much as we can about him! These few years are called the ministry of Jesus. We have already seen how difficult it is to learn anything definite about dates in the life of Jesus. The Gospel writers were not interested in putting down these details because they were not as interested as we are in them, and because those for whom these books were written knew the facts anyway. There seemed to be no point in repeating them. As we turn to the ministry of Jesus, we find the same problem in dating which we ran into in both the birth and the baptism of Jesus. Once again we must say we really do not know the exact time when this important phase of his life began or ended.

The Synoptic Gospels tell us that Jesus began his preaching in Galilee after the arrest of John the Baptist (Matthew 4:12-17; Mark 1:14; Luke 4:14-15). The Gospel of John, however, tells us that Jesus spent a good length of time in Judea, a fact the Synoptics do not mention (John 3:22-24). In the Gospel of John, Jesus is pictured as beginning to preach almost at once, while the Baptist was still alive (John 1:35-39; 4:1). These are confusing contradictions, worth noting in view of the increasing interest in John the Baptist and his possible influence on Christianity. Judea was the area from which John the Baptist came.

It is possible that the Gospel of John preserved for us a fact which may be of great importance. Perhaps after his baptism Jesus went to Judea where he worked with the disciples of John the Baptist. It may be that only after the arrest of John the Baptist did Jesus start his own independent ministry. There was obviously a lapse of time between the temptation and the beginning of the Galilean ministry. It seems logical that Jesus became for a short time a follower of John the Baptist. It was John who baptized Jesus, and it was from among John's disciples that some of the earliest followers of Jesus were recruited. When John the Baptist was arrested and then beheaded, Jesus continued along the path John had started.

In the end, of course, it was Jesus who so inspired men that a new religion was born; but in the beginning it could well have been John the Baptist who inspired Jesus.

As for the length of time during which Jesus preached and taught, there is no certain way of knowing. It is possible to go through the Gospels picking out references to "green grass" or "the harvest" or references to holidays and then to conjecture how many months have passed. This is, however, a dubious way to determine a date. As we have seen, the materials in the Gospels are mixed up. There is no assurance that we would not be taking two accounts of the same event and thus counting two years when we should be counting one. The estimates vary from one year to four, with most scholars agreeing that the ministry was about three years long. The Gospels all indicate that the ministry was short, but one or two years seem too short for all that is related to have happened, and a very short time for any man, no matter how great, to have made the impact that Jesus did.

The Disciples

Early in the ministry of Jesus, we hear about his Disciples. Apparently there was quite a large number of them, drawn from every walk of life. There were some who had heard Jesus preach, and who agreed with what he had to say, so that they gathered about him whenever he appeared to preach. There were others who had heard about him and wanted to hear him in person. The word disciples or "followers" is used for those large numbers of people who did not necessarily follow Jesus everywhere he went, but who formed the crowds in the spot where he happened to be. The word is used much in the way we use the word "follower." We often say that a great preacher has a large following, but by this we would not mean that these people are literally following the preacher around! The word is also used to refer to the band of twelve men, specially chosen, who actually accompanied Jesus. The Twelve were the close associates of Jesus, but probably there were always others going from place to place with Jesus. There seem to have been women among them (see Luke 8:1-3). When the word "disciple" is used to mean the Twelve, it should be capitalized and then there will be no confusion.

Another word which is used in the New Testament and often confused with "disciple" is the word "apostle." Sometimes apostle means Disciple, one of the Twelve specially chosen men, and at other times it refers to anyone who went out on a missionary trip. The word means "one sent out." At other times the word is limited to those who had a special charge from Jesus. One of those who called himself an apostle was Paul, and he was criticized for calling himself this because he never knew Jesus. Nevertheless, he insisted that he had this right because he had had a vision of Jesus which gave him special authority.

There are four lists of the Disciples in the New Testament (Mark 3:16-18; Matthew 10:2-4; Luke 6:14-16; Acts 1:13). These lists have some minor variations and the order of the names listed is not the same in all four, but they are obviously the same list. Why there were twelve, we can only guess. The most obvious reason would be because of the twelve tribes of Israel. The appointment of twelve would indicate that this movement of Jesus was to include all of Israel—all twelve tribes. The number twelve was also a number which was often used as a "round" number, as we still use it: "an even dozen" for example.

Why these men came to follow Jesus, and how they were appointed to the Twelve, we do not really know. The Gospels tell of the calling of five of the Disciples, but of the others they say nothing. We can read of the calling of Peter, Andrew, James and John in Mark 1:16-20. Matthew (4:18-22) adds nothing to Mark's version, but Luke (5:1-11) tells a more elaborate story. Read Mark and Luke.

> Do you think it possible that these fishermen would
> have left their work so abruptly to follow Jesus?
>
> What possible explanation of this could there be?

We are told, also, of the call of Matthew or Levi which occurred not long after the call of the first four. Read Mark
2:13-14; Matthew 9:9; Luke 5:27-32. Remembering that
the Pharisees felt that one should be religious by observing
the rules and regulations of religion and keeping oneself ritually clean, can you understand why they would be shocked
that Jesus was eating with sinners?

> Why do you suppose tax collectors were included
> among the "unclean"?
>
> What do you think of Jesus' answer to the Pharisees'
> criticism? (Luke 5:31-32)
>
> Can you put this in your own words?

Another example of Jesus' teaching which was in contradiction to the feelings of many of the people of his time concerning the observation of religion is found in all three Synoptics, but the clearest version is in Mark 2:23-28.

> Give some modern examples of religious practice where
> it might be appropriate to remark, "the sabbath was
> made for man, not man for the sabbath."

Of the calling of the other Disciples, we know nothing.
Actually we are told little about any of the Twelve except
Peter, James and John. This does not mean that all twelve
were not of equal importance. The Gospels are short and selective, so that we cannot assume that just because the others
are not mentioned, that they did nothing. It is more than
likely that all of them played a large role in establishing the
religion of Jesus. We get a glimpse of their role in Mark 6:7-
13. Read this passage. The parallel passages in Matthew and
Luke are much the same. If you would like to compare them,
they are in Matthew 10:1, 5, 7-11 and Luke 9:1-5.

> What do you think "gave them authority over the un-
> clean spirits" means?

How were the Disciples supposed to live while they
were out on their preaching mission?

If there were people in these towns who would be
friendly to such wandering preachers as the Disciples, who do you think they might be?

It is obvious that men would not be sent out to preach
without first having had some training. This would be especially true of those from such diversified backgrounds as
the Disciples. Exactly how Jesus trained them we do not
know, but there are many instances throughout the Gospels
where he took his Disciples aside and instructed them. As we
read various sections of the Gospels, we can take note of this.
Of course, the mere fact that the Twelve were living with
Jesus and accompanying him while he preached and taught,
would give these men, by example, an education in what was
expected of them. We should not think of the Disciples as
having suddenly decided to follow Jesus, and then immediately having been sent out to preach. They undoubtedly had
some contact with Jesus before they were "called" and they
must have had some kind of qualifications which made Jesus
choose them for the important work he wanted them to do.
Also, after he had chosen them, he must have given them
careful instructions in what they were to preach and how
they were to behave. This process is seen only dimly in the
Gospels, but the indications are that this was the way in
which the Disciples were trained. The whole Christian movement depended on these men after the death of Jesus. They
were equal to the task and they carried on the work of their
Master ably, effectively and well. These were no ordinary
men!

The Teaching

In spite of the vagueness of our knowledge about the life
of Jesus, the amazing fact remains that he commands our at-

tention and serious study so many centuries after his death. The reason for this obviously lies in something besides the mere events in his career. As we look over the Gospels we see that large parts of them are concerned not with events but with teachings and deeds. Exactly when or where these words were spoken or these deeds performed were not of concern to the writers. We can observe many pithy sayings, longer paragraphs of teaching, conversations, stories or parables, and many instances of marvelous happenings and of healings. It is within these teachings and deeds that we may find the key to the importance which Jesus had for history. It is easy to become so interested in the events of Jesus' life that we forget the teaching, and yet the importance of Jesus as a man lies in his teachings. To understand what he taught is to understand his greatness. We cannot possibly consider all the teachings, all the parables or all the miracles in this short book. We are going to select a few of them to study. First, the Sermon on the Mount.

The Sermon on the Mount

The Sermon on the Mount is the best known and longest collection of the sayings of Jesus. It is found in Matthew 5, 6, 7. Before we turn to it, recall the process through which the teaching and preaching of Jesus went before it was written down by the Gospel writers. This was discussed in detail in Chapter Four. We should review it briefly now. It might also be well to reread the second section of Chapter Five which tells about the various religious ideas of the time of Jesus, because the Sermon on the Mount will make a great deal more sense if you understand thoroughly the religious views of the people to whom these things were said.

Turn to Matthew and glance through the three chapters

Rohlfs (1849 – 1938), woodcut, 1926, The Sermon on the Mount
Courtesy of New York Public Library, Prints Division

containing the Sermon on the Mount. Compare it with Luke 6:17-49 which contains a somewhat briefer version of the same collection of sayings. Notice that the setting of the Sermon is different in Luke.

There are scholars who think that the Lukan version is the older one and more authentic—in other words, closer to the actual words of Jesus. This may be so, and we must constantly bear in mind that what we are reading has passed through many hands and many minds, so that in neither version are we reading the exact words of Jesus. We may be reading what people thought Jesus said, or what they wished he had said, or what they hoped he had said. But we *are* reading those words which have influenced mankind for generations even though they may not be exactly as Jesus stated them. There are some parts of the Sermon on the Mount which we know come from the early Christian church, and it is quite likely that a large part of it has been influenced by the needs of that church. There are some basic principles stated here which must have come from Jesus himself.

Look through the Sermon again in more detail and make a list of the topics or general categories the compiler has used. Don't break this down into topics which are too small, but make a list of headings under which the various sayings are collected. Put this list aside. We will refer to it later.

Read Matthew 5:3-12 which is called the Beatitudes, meaning the "blesseds."

According to these verses what kind of people are part of the kingdom of heaven?

Does the passage indicate whether the kingdom is present or future?

Compare these Beatitudes with those in Luke 6:20-23 and the Woes in Luke 6:24-26.

To whom does the last Beatitude refer, in both versions?

Read Matthew 5:13-16.

Who are the "salt of the earth" (Matthew 5:13)?

Who is the "light of the world" (Matthew 5:14)?

Matthew 5:17-20 serves as a general introduction to the sections following. Note that in verse 20, Jesus emphasized that he meant his followers to adhere to a greater righteousness than that of the Scribes and Pharisees. However, verses 18-19 seem to contradict the nonconforming attitude which Jesus exhibited in such a remark as "the sabbath was made for man not man for the sabbath." Most scholars think that these verses were added later in order to answer a criticism which was made of Jesus by the strictly conforming Jewish group. Read these verses (17-20) again and state what the criticisms might have been.

The rest of Chapter Five presents *a new interpretation of ethical standards* to that which was currently held. Jesus quoted some of the Old Testament commandments, and then went on to expound his view of how the commandments must be obeyed. Read 5:21-22. Do you think that if you call one of your friends "you fool" you have done something really bad?

In order to understand why Jesus made such a point of this, think for a moment about how fights start. Have you ever started a friendly little argument and had it grow into a full-scale fight? Have you ever said something to someone which was mean, and had that person get hurt or angry so that you were no longer friends? Is it true, as Jesus seems to indicate, that killing and calling someone a fool are equally serious, if one considers as primary not the deed but the inner attitude of the person doing the killing or name-calling? Verses 23 and 24 are another teaching with a slightly different meaning. State this meaning clearly.

Verses 25-26 are open to more than one interpretation. Did Jesus mean that a person should not permit another to settle his differences? In other words should all disputes be settled "out of court"? Suppose we do not take this passage literally, but as an allegory of the Judgment Day. Interpreted this way, it would mean that those who bear malice against a fellow man will not fare well at the Final Judgment.

It is also possible that these two verses come from the period of the early church when it was downright dangerous to be a Christian, so that from a practical point of view it was foolish to get oneself into the position of being brought into court, for inevitably, whether you were guilty or not, the judgment would go against you.

Which interpretation of this passage do you like best?

Why do you like it?

The next section (verses 27-30) concerns the commandment about adultery.

What change did Jesus make in the interpretation of this commandment?

Verses 29 and 30 have been interpreted by some literally. If you do something with your hand which is wrong, you should cut it off! Others think that Jesus often exaggerated to make a point and that he had a sense of humor. From this viewpoint, he was saying, "Watch yourself" and "Don't make excuses."

Divorce is dealt with in verses 31-32. Read Luke 16:18 where the material is stated even more bluntly. Some people think that the statement "except on the ground of unchastity" in Matthew was added later to make this teaching less difficult. It is interesting to note that in our modern world there are those who accept the Lukan version of this teaching and do not recognize divorce for any reason whatsoever, for example the Roman Catholic Church; and there are those who accept the Matthean version and will recognize divorce and permit remarriage of the innocent party, but not of the guilty one, as in the Episcopal Church. Still others take the position that since this teaching was given in an age when women had few if any rights, and therefore no way of supporting themselves unless they had husbands, this was a teaching intended to help protect women from husbands who might just shove them aside. There are people who say that this teaching is out-of-date now and does not apply in the modern world. These people leave the whole matter of whether divorced people can be married in the church to the discretion of the minister. If he thinks the couple is serious and will make a real effort to build a good marriage, he will marry them. Why not discuss this with your own minister to see what standards he sets for performing marriages of divorced persons? How you feel about this problem of divorce?

Verses 33-37 discuss the matter of swearing; that is, swearing in a sense of taking an oath. The third commandment, "You shall not take the name of the Lord your God in vain" (Deuteronomy 5:11) has often been interpreted to mean that you should never swear an oath, whereas it actually says not to take the name of God *in vain*. If you mean it, it is all right to swear! There were those, however, who practiced swearing and then failed to live up to the obligation which they had incurred by evading the oath. They would say they had failed to include one phrase, for example, so the oath was not valid. Others would swear by something besides God in order to have an oath which was not forbidden by religious law (Matthew 5:34). See what Jesus said about these practices (verse 37). This view is expressed even more concisely in a book from the early church. Read James 5:12.

> What do you think of the simple command of Jesus that you say "yes" or "no" and that this should be sufficient?
>
> What is the difference between this kind of swearing and the kind we hear in everyday life which we call profanity?
>
> Which person would you respect more, one who promises to do something by saying simply, "Yes, I will" or someone who prefaces what he says by a whole string of "swearwords"?

There have been two interpretations of this passage: one which interprets it to mean that no oath at any time is proper, even, for example, in court. Others interpret this to mean that swearing is all right, provided the oath is honored and that the person does what he swears to do.

In verses 38-42 we find a well-known passage which has influenced many, while baffling others. Jesus quoted the Old Testament command that harm should be repaid in exactly the same degree that it was received. If you put someone's eye out, you should have yours put out in return. Today this seems cruel, but it was mild compared to what had happened at the time the command was written (c. 1000 B.C.). Tribal revenge was a terrifying thing. If a member of one tribe injured a member of another, the fellow tribesmen of the injured party would often feel obliged to take revenge in excess of the damage done. The commandment in Exodus 21:24 is to make things fair. Only as much as was done in injury can be exacted in payment. Jesus went further, and disagreed with this.

> What did he say you should do if someone injures you?
> Do you think that the principle proposed here of overcoming evil with good is practical in everyday life?
> Would it work, for example, with a bully?
> What results do you think such a course of action would have?

Some people feel that this principle of "passive resistance" is good for interpersonal relations but not in international affairs, because the principle presupposes that one can face the person who has done the injury to you. The argument is that nations are too impersonal and that, therefore, other means must be found to correct injuries between them. There are others, however, who feel that this principle is one which should be carried out in all relationships of man to man and that it is important to live up to it even to the extent of refusing to go to war. What do you think? Can you give an example of passive resistance in our own day?

The last section of Chapter 5 is, in a way, an expansion of the previous section.

> What logic did Jesus use in attempting to show the validity of the command to love your enemies?
> What do you think of it?

In Matthew 6:1-18 is a collection of *sayings* which are *concerned with proper religious practices*. Beginning with verse 1, read carefully each section and think of a modern parallel. For example, verse 1 speaks of "practicing your piety before men in order to be seen by them." Have you ever observed anyone who did this, perhaps by arriving in church late to be sure to be seen; or by being the first to rise for a hymn, or in other ways? Consider in the same way each of the practices which are included in this section: alms (you might translate this "give to charity"), prayer, and festivals. Try to state in one sentence what Jesus says in this section about the practice of religion.

Verses 9-13 include the *Lord's Prayer*. We have already had occasion to mention this in the section about John the Baptist. Much could be written about this prayer; in fact, much has been! If one tries to understand all of the background of thought that lies behind it, and the various interpretations which can be given it in our modern age, a great many pages would be needed. Perhaps this is unnecessary, for some of the simplest ideas are the most profound. Here is a prayer that is repeated frequently. It means a great deal to many people. Others, however, repeat this prayer so often and so automatically that it becomes a "heaping up of empty phrases" (verse 7). Read the prayer through carefully as though you had never seen it before. Take it line by line and put it into your own words.

Is there a difference between what the prayer means to you and what it must have meant to Jesus? For example, explain the phrase, "Thy Kingdom Come." The footnote in the Revised Standard Version for verse 13 tells us that originally the word "evil" was "the evil one" or the devil. What is the difference if we read it this way? The footnote also explains that the last phrase which is often used in saying the prayer is included in a few of the ancient sources, but not all. It is generally agreed that this phrase is one which was added to the prayer sometime during the years of the early Christian church. Therefore, it is not included in the text of the Revised Standard Version.

Do you think that it adds anything to the prayer?

If so, *what* does it add?

Verses 19-34 include sayings about one's attitudes toward earthly possessions and one's attitudes toward the life of this world. Be careful not to be too literal when reading these passages. For example, in verses 19-21 was Jesus referring to real treasure when he spoke of "treasure in heaven"? Did he not mean, rather, the development of the spiritual life as contrasted with the preoccupation with the accumulation of worldly wealth? Think about these verses and see if you can translate them into your own words. You might try to think of two people, or types of people, who would personify the two ways of life here described.

The rest of Chapter Six is composed of further sayings on this same topic. Among them are some of the most often quoted of the words of Jesus. They are also among the most important. In order to understand them, it is necessary to read each one carefully and then think about its meaning. It helps to put the sayings into your own words as well as you can. Summarize the essential thought of these verses in one sentence.

Chapter Seven begins with a saying on *judging others*. We might use the word criticize in place of judge to see more clearly what this saying means. Verses 3-5 expand 1-2 in a humorous way. Put this section into your own words.

Verse 6 is considered by most authorities as either a later addition put into the Sermon by a member of a group who believed in making Christianity exclusive, or else a garbled version of an original saying. Contrast this verse with those we have just read in verses 1-5. Give reasons for believing that this is not one of the sayings of Jesus.

Verses 7-11 are probably referring to the relationship of man and God in prayer. Try interpreting the passage in this way. Try to think of others ways of interpreting it. Verse 12 contains the famous *Golden Rule*. In both Judaism and Confucianism this same idea is expressed but in the negative:

"Do not do to others what you would have them not do to you." It has been argued that the latter saying is better. On the other hand, there have been those who have named the negative form of this rule the "Silver Rule," indicating that it was less to be desired than the "Golden Rule" of Jesus. Much can be said on both sides of this question. Make a list of the advantages of the positive form of the rule over the negative. Now make a list of the advantages of the negative rule over the positive. Choose the form you like best, and state reasons for your choice.

Verses 13-14 probably mean that few will be part of the Kingdom of God. However, the general idea presented here could be applied to other aims in life.

Can you think of some of these aims?

How can one tell whether a man is a false prophet or not (verses 15-20)? Could this saying be applied to other than prophets? Interpret this passage in modern terms.

Verses 21-23 reiterate *the inwardness of religion* and the essential factor in it of true devotion to God. What did Jesus say men can do and still not be part of the Kingdom of God?

Verses 24-27 form a fitting conclusion to this collection of sayings. Put the paragraph into your own words, and explain why you agree or disagree.

Now that we have concluded our survey of the Sermon on the Mount look again at the list of topics into which you divided the Sermon when you first started reading it. Would you make any changes in it now that you have read the whole section thoroughly?

Put under each heading the one sentence which sums up the teaching of that section. When you do this, you will have a concise summary of the principal teachings of the Sermon on the Mount. Has your study changed any of your ideas? In what way?

Do you think that it is one of the greatest pieces of religious writing of all times?

If you do not, can you understand why many people think that it is?

Since there is so much to understand in this section, it

would be a good idea to reread your summary and to think about it some more. Look back over it and remember all the places where there are differing interpretations and all the places where you gained new ideas from trying to understand the sayings and from choosing among the possible meanings.

The Sermon on the Mount is only a part of what Jesus taught. We have looked at it in detail because it contains some of the most famous sayings of Jesus. In addition, we must look at some of the other teachings of Jesus which are not sayings, but are longer and more picturesque. They are called parables and we will select a few for special study.

The Parables

One of the outstanding characteristics of the teaching of Jesus is the profusion of illustrations taken from the common life of his time. Many of his illustrations are timeless; they were taken from nature and are the same for us today as they were for those who listened almost 2000 years ago. Such simple illustrations as those we read in the Sermon on the Mount are characteristic of his teaching. Consider the statement, "look at the birds of the air: they neither sow nor reap nor gather into barns"; into our minds comes the picture of birds flying through the air, and the thought that they do not have to earn a living is something we may not have considered. Such illustrations make the teaching lively and interesting. If we could have heard Jesus speak, or if we had a transcription of one of his talks or sermons, we would no doubt find it fascinating.

Some of the illustrations which Jesus used are considered in a special category. These are the parables, and they are usually longer than one or two sentences. They are stories which are told in order to make a point clear. The listener is not always sure until the end what the point is going to be, but when the story is complete, it is quite clear. These stories were told originally in answer to a question or in a context. Some of the parables are difficult to interpret because most of these questions and settings have been lost. In its setting the parable was clear and easy to understand. A parable is not an allegory; an allegory is often obscure since every little detail stands for something. An allegory is symbolic, whereas a parable is a comparison with a point.

There are many parables in the Gospels. A list of those we do not have time to study will be found at the end of this section. First let us look at the "Parable of the Sower." This is found in Mark 4:2-9, in Matthew 13:1-9 and in Luke 8:4-8. Luke has a slightly shorter version than the other two, but it is substantially the same. Mark and Matthew are almost exactly the same. Turn to Mark and read the whole parable. This story uses a figure which was a common sight to those who lived in the time of Jesus. Most of us are not familiar with a sower, but we have seen pictures of such a man walking through the fields with a bag of seed under one arm from which handfuls are taken and flung out over the field. Obviously this method of planting seed was not as efficient as our modern methods because much more of the seed was wasted. Put the meaning of this parable into your own words.

The following verses give an explanation of this against which you can check your interpretation. Read Mark 4:10-20. Do you agree with Mark in verses 11-12 that Jesus spoke in parables in order that those outside the chosen few would be confused by them?

Who is the sower?

Who is the word?

Read Mark 4:30-32, "The Parable of the Mustard Seed." What does this parable tell us about the Kingdom of God?

A much longer parable is that of "The Prodigal Son." This

is found in Luke 15: 11-32 but not in the other two gospels. Read it all the way through.

Describe your feelings about the younger son.

Do you think the father was right to take him back again?

Do you think that the older son was correct in protesting?

What do you think of the father's answer to this protest?

Remember that this is a parable. See if you can translate it into its religious terms. State carefully the main point of the parable. To check your interpretation, read another parable on the same subject in Luke 15:3-7. Luke 15:8-10 also makes the same point. Discuss this parable again in the light of its religious meanings.

Another well-known parable is "The Parable of the Good Samaritan" (Luke 10:30-36). This is found only in Luke. After you have read it, translate it into modern terms so that the full impact of the message comes out.

The following facts will help you do this if you are not already familiar with them. The Samaritans were a people of the same background and ethnic origin as the Jews who lived in the central part of Palestine, but who several centuries previous to Jesus' time had been conquered and had intermarried with the conquerors. They had also continued their religion as it had been in those days and had not accepted the later books of the Old Testament as had the Jews of the time of Jesus. For a long time, therefore, they had been looked down upon by the orthodox Jews as "half-breeds" and "heretics" who were to be despised and avoided. No orthodox Jew would associate with them. The Levites were the priestly aristocracy of Jerusalem. They considered themselves, and were considered by others, to be "better." Also, because of their position in life, they had to live by a great many rules to keep themselves ritually clean. The same would be true of the priest who was set apart because of his vocation. Think of representatives of modern groups whose names could be substituted for Samaritan, Levite and priest. For example, you might substitute the name of an unpopular minority group for Samaritan, one of the town's leading citizens for Levite and a religious leader for priest. Substituting these names, or others you may choose, reread the parable.

"The Parable of the Great Banquet" is a dramatic one (Luke 14:16-24). Read this and interpret it in your own words. Compare the version, apparently of the same parable, in Matthew 22:1-10 where it has been allegorized. From even a quick reading it is obvious that the whole tone of Matthew's version is different, and there are things which are hard to understand if we read it as a parable. As an allegory it makes sense: God is the king, Jesus is the son, the Jews are the invited guests, the Old Testament prophets are the servants and the banquet and wedding hall are the Kingdom of God.

Which version do you think is older, the allegory or the parable?

Make a one sentence summary of each of these parables. Add this summary to that which you made for the Sermon on the Mount.

Here is a list of some other well-known parables, which you say may read if you wish. All are well known, and are often referred to in literature. What do they add to your understanding of the meaning of the Kingdom of God? To other understandings?

"Laborers in the Vineyard," Matthew 20: 1-16.
"Foolish Maidens," Matthew 25: 1-13.
"Talents," Matthew 25: 13-30.
"Sheep and Goats." Matthew 25: 31-46.
"Rich Man and Lazarus" Luke 16: 19-31.
"Pharisee and the Publican" Luke 18: 9-14.

The Miracles

Mark 5: 39-42
[39] And when he had entered, he said to them, "Why do you make a tumult and weep? The child is not dead but sleeping." [40] And they

laughed at him. But he put them all outside, and took the child's father and mother and those who were with him, and went in where the child was. [41] Taking her by the hand he said to her, "Tal'itha cu'mi"; which means, "Little girl, I say to you, arise." [42] And immediately the girl got up and walked; for she was twelve years old. And immediately they were overcome with amazement.

Mark 6:48b-50

And about the fourth watch of the night he came to them, walking on the sea. He meant to pass by them, [49] but when they saw him walking on the sea they thought it was a ghost, and cried out; [50] for they all saw him, and were terrified.

> Did these things really happen?
> Is it possible for a girl to be raised from the dead, or for a man to walk on the water?

Included in the Gospels are many marvelous events which we call miracles. For some, the miracles are of primary importance in testifying to the uniqueness of Jesus and to his special relationship with God. To others, the miracles form a stumbling block, for they seem to make Jesus a magical wonder-worker and so to detract from the impact of his ethical teaching. Sometimes people defend the miracles in every detail, insisting that unless you believe them, you cannot hold Jesus in the esteem with which he must be held. Others insist equally staunchly that if you accept the miraculous in the Gospels, you are accepting superstition from another age, and that the importance of the life of Jesus does not lie in them. These are the extreme positions. Most people accept something in between. Before we can consider the meaning of any of the miracles, we must stop to consider just what we mean by the word miracle.

In the days of primitive man before there was any scientific knowledge, every event which could not be explained by man was a miracle. A miracle was simply a wonderful or awesome or fearful event of which men did not know the cause. Thus the primitive world abounded in miracles. As man's knowledge of his world expanded, the number of "miracles" lessened. Natural phenomena before which, in former days, man would have stood in awe were now understood and no longer feared, worshipped or appeased.

Pretend that you are living in the earliest era of the life of man on earth. You have little knowledge of the world around you. You have practical knowledge, but no theoretical knowledge. In other words, you know that it rains from time to time, but you have no idea why. You know that sometimes great streaks of fire flash through the sky during a storm, but you have no idea as to what causes them. You may have observed that rain helps make things grow. What would you do during a drought to try to make it rain? Imagine how you would feel when it started to rain. How would you try to prevent the lightning from striking you or near you? How do you think you would feel about lightning? Think of some other examples of things which you, as a primitive man, would find terribly frightening or awe-inspiring for which today you would have an explanation.

As time went on and man's culture developed, there came into being a belief in natural order. Men discovered a consistency in the way nature worked, and so discovered what we call natural law. God, or the gods, became in the minds of men the power which controlled the natural forces, i.e., the *super*natural. A miracle became the interference of the supernatural beings in the natural order of things. For a long time it was believed that God or the gods could interfere at will. A miracle was an unusual event or a strange happening for which man had no explanation. He explained it as being the work of the supernatural.

As modern science developed, the idea of God as a power behind the universe who intervened in the natural order from time to time became difficult for modern man to accept. Underlying our modern scientific approach to the universe is the assumption that there are laws which govern the universe and that these always operate in the same way. Those events and occurrences which previous generations would have called a miracle, modern man accepts as something we do not yet understand. Many people accept this scientific approach and believe in God, not as a being who interferes in the natural order of things, but as a force behind the universe. They see God as the creator of the universe, the instigator of the laws governing it. According to such a belief, God as well as man obeys those laws, and there is no such thing as a miracle in the old sense.

It is this conflict between the idea of a universe which can be counted on to operate according to set laws and the idea that through divine intervention these set laws can be set aside which causes difficulty in interpreting and understanding the miracles in the New Testament. If you believe in a God who can, at will, set aside the natural law and do something contrary to it, then the idea of a miracle is no problem. You can accept all miracles at face value. On the other hand, if you hold to the belief that things that cannot be explained are those things which we do not yet understand, you will reject the idea of a miracle in a supernatural sense completely.

This problem becomes important when we read the New Testament narration of the life of Jesus. Here we are reading a record of a life which was written in a prescientific age. The Gospel writers believed in a God who could, and did, intervene at will in the affairs of men. Their explanation of some illnesses, especially those we call mental illnesses, was that the sick person was inhabited by a demon or an evil spirit. These could be driven out, if you knew how to do it, and this would be a miracle.

There was nothing which would indicate to them that a man could not walk on the water if God was with him. Thus, a man like Jesus, who had such a special relationship with God, could do anything. In fact, in the times in which the Gospels were written, a religious leader who could not do miracles would not be considered worth following. Jesus' followers undoubtedly exaggerated some stories to prove his worth. It was assumed by those who followed Jesus that he had power from God to do marvelous things. Some of those marvelous things he probably did do; some of them his followers thought he did, through misunderstanding or misinterpretation; and others he did not do. Those he did not do found their way into the Gospels in a credulous age both because of exaggeration and the hazards of word of mouth transmission.

We shall select a few of the miracles to look at in detail, and as we do so, some of the things we have just been considering will become clearer.

There are two main types of miracles which were reported to have been performed by Jesus: the miracles of healing and the nature miracles. The miracles of healing were those in which Jesus healed someone of a disease or a mental illness, or, in one or two instances, raised someone from the dead. The nature miracles are those which involve not people but inanimate objects. We shall consider examples of both kinds.

The Miracles of Healing

There are many examples in the Gospels of healing miracles. We will consider only four of them which are representative of the others. Turn to Mark 5:1-20 and read the entire passage. This story of healing reflects the beliefs of the first century.

What did the author of the Gospel think was wrong with the man Jesus healed?

From a modern point of view, accepting the facts as stated in the Gospel at face value, what do you think may have been wrong with the man?

How did the Gospel writer think the man was cured by Jesus?

How do you think the man was cured by Jesus?

What do you think about the explanation that the evil spirits went into the swine?

Can you explain what may have happened to the swine?

Why were the people so afraid of Jesus after he had cured this man?

What was Jesus' explanation of how the man was cured?

Read Mark 5:21-43. Note that there are two miracles in this passage. We shall look first at the story of the woman with the hemorrhage. Compare the three versions.

Mark 5:25-34

25 And there was a woman who had had a flow of blood for twelve years, 26 and who had suffered much under many physicians, and had spent all that she had, and was no better but rather grew worse. 27 She had heard the reports about Jesus, and came up behind him in the crowd and touched his garment. 28 For she said, "If I touch even his garments, I shall be made well." 29 And immediately the hemorrhage ceased; and she felt in her body that she was healed of her disease. 30 And Jesus, perceiving in himself that power had gone forth from him, immediately turned about in the crowd, and said, "Who touched my garments?" 31 And his disciples said to him, " You see the crowd pressing around you, and yet you say, 'Who touched me?' " 32 And he looked around to see who had done it. 33 But the woman, knowing what had been done to her, came in fear and trembling and fell down before him, and told him the whole truth. 34 And he said to her, "Daughter, your faith has made you well; go in peace, and be healed of your disease."

Matthew 9:20-22

20 And behold, a woman who had suffered from a hemorrhage for twelve years came up behind him and touched the fringe of his garment; 21 for she said to herself, "If I only touch his garment, I shall be made well." 22 Jesus turned, and seeing her he said, "Take heart, daughter; your faith has made you well." And instantly the woman was made well.

Luke 8:43-48

As he went, the people pressed round him. 43 And a woman who had had a flow of blood for twelve years and could not be healed by any one, [44] came up behind him, and touched the fringe of his garment; and immediately her flow of blood ceased. [45] And Jesus said, "Who was it that touched me?" When all denied it, Peter said, "Master, the multitudes surround you and press upon you!" [46] But Jesus said, "Some one touched me; for I perceive that power has gone forth from me." [47] And when the woman saw that she was not hidden, she came trembling, and falling down before him declared in the presence of all the people why she had touched him, and how she had been immediately healed. [48] And he said to her, "Daughter, your faith has made you well; go in peace."

What did Jesus say, in all three versions was the cause of the woman's cure?

Do you think this would be possible?

What additional element of cure do Mark and Luke include in their versions?

What do you think of Mark's opinion of doctors (verse 26)?

The story of the raising of Jairus' daughter is substantially the same in all three Gospels. Read the Markan version (Mark 5:21-24; 35-43) carefully. In your own words, according to the Gospel, what happened? Do you think this is possible? Give your reasons for answering as you do. Can you think of an explanation for this miracle which would satisfy a scientifically minded person? Take your clue from the story itself: what did Jesus say was wrong with the girl?

Now read this other story:

Mark 9:14-29

14 And when they came to the disciples, they saw a great crowd about them, and scribes arguing with them. [15] And immediately all the crowd, when they saw him, were greatly amazed, and ran up to him and greeted him. [16] And he asked them, "What are you discussing with them?" [17] And one of the crowd answered him, "Teacher, I brought my son to you, for he has a dumb spirit; [18] and wherever it seizes him, it dashes him down; and he foams and grinds his teeth and becomes rigid; and I asked your disciples to cast it out, and they were not able." [19] And he answerd them, "O faithless generation, how long am I to be with you? How long am I to bear with you? Bring him to

me." 20 And they brought the boy to him; and when the spirit saw him, immediately it convulsed the boy, and he fell on the ground and rolled about, foaming at the mouth. 21 And Jesus asked his father, "How long has he had this?" And he said, "From childhood. 22 And it has often cast him into the fire and into the water, to destroy him; but if you can do anything, have pity on us and help us." 23 And Jesus said to him, "If you can! All things are possible to him who believes." 24 Immediately the father of the child cried out and said, "I believe; help my unbelief!" 25 And when Jesus saw that a crowd came running together, he rebuked the unclean spirit, saying to it, "You dumb and deaf spirit, I command you, come out of him, and never enter him again." 26 And after crying out and convulsing him terribly, it came out, and the boy was like a corpse; so that most of them said, "He is dead." 27 But Jesus took him by the hand and lifted him up, and he arose. 28 And when he had entered the house, his disciples asked him privately, "Why could we not cast it out?" 29 And he said to them, "This kind cannot be driven out by anything but prayer."

Matthew 17:14-18

14 And when they came to the crowd, a man came up to him and kneeling before him said, 15 "Lord, have mercy on my son, for he is an epileptic and he suffers terribly; for often he falls into the fire, and often into the water. 16 And I brought him to your disciples, and they could not heal him." 17 And Jesus answered, "O faithless and perverse generation, how long am I to be with you? How long am I to bear with you? Bring him here to me." 18 And Jesus rebuked him, and the demon came out of him, and the boy was cured instantly.

Luke 9:37-43

37 On the next day, when they had come down from the mountain, a great crowd met him. 38 And behold, a man from the crowd cried, "Teacher, I beg you to look upon my son, for he is my only child; 39 and behold, a spirit seizes him, and he suddenly cries out; it convulses him till he foams, and shatters him, and will hardly leave him. 40 And I begged your disciples to cast it out, but they could not." 41 Jesus answered, "O faithless and perverse generation, how long am I to be with you and bear with you? Bring your son here." 42 While he was coming, the demon tore him and convulsed him. But Jesus rebuked the unclean spirit, and healed the boy, and gave him back to his father. 43 And all were astonished at the majesty of God.

What was wrong with the boy (Matthew 17:15)?
What explanation of this illness was made by the Gos-

pel writers (Mark 9:17 and 25; Matthew 17:18; Luke 9:39 and 42)?

Would we give this explanation?

What reason is given in the three accounts for the Disciples' inability to heal the boy?

What does the statement of the father mean: "I believe, help my unbelief"?

After having read these four miracles, and thinking of the introduction to miracles, what is *your* attitude toward them? Here are some questions which may help you think this through.

Do you think that these miracles were brought about by the direct intervention of God as suggested, for example, in Luke 9:43?

Do you think that there are people who have been given special power by God so that they can perform miracles, as suggested in Mark 5:30?

If your answer to both these questions is negative (if it is, think through your reasons for rejecting these ideas) what do you think is the explanation for Jesus' reputation as a healer?

What do you think of the idea that faith can heal, as set forth in the healing of the woman with the hemorrhage and in the healing of the epileptic boy?

Sum up, in one sentence, the teaching the Gospels present through the healing miracles.

The Nature Miracles

One of the best-known nature miracles is "The Feeding of the Five Thousand." You can read this in Mark 6:32-44, in Matthew 14:13-21, in Luke 9:11-17 or in John 6:5-15. The feeding of the *four* thousand which is considered by most scholars to be a variation on the other is found in Mark 8:1-10 and in Matthew 15:32-39. If you read and compare these various versions of what was obviously the same event, you will note that there is little difference among them. They all tell substantially the same story. It is interesting to note, too, that this is the only miracle which is told in all four Gospels. Our problem arises when we try to interpret it.

According to the story, Jesus took a small amount of food and multiplied it so that it fed a vast number of people. But what is the point of this? Why should Jesus want to do this? How does this event fit in with the conception of the role which he seems to have had in the temptation? Following the feeding of the four thousand in Mark 8: 1-10 there seems to be a direct contradiction to the seeming reason for the feeding. Read Mark 8:12. Another indication of this attitude on the part of Jesus that he would not do magic, and that he would not give "signs" in order to convince people he had a special mission, or a special relationship with God is seen in Matthew 16:1-4. If we accept the interpretation which these passages would indicate, that Jesus shunned wonder-working, then how are we to interpret the feeding of the five thousand? Try to interpret it for yourself.

Some think that this was a symbolic act. Jesus broke the bread as a symbol of the Last Supper which later became the Communion in the Christian Church. The feeding, then, would be symbolic of the spread of the "good news" which is what the word Gospel means. This interpretation is strengthened by the fact that John, although he tells the story in much the same form as do the Synoptics, interprets it in different and typically Johanine way by following it with a description of Jesus as the "bread of life." "I am the bread of life; he who comes to me shall not hunger, and he who believes in me shall never thirst" (John 6:35). Adherents of this point of view also bring to our attention that nowhere do the Gospels actually say there was enough made from the few loaves to feed the five thousand. We merely surmise this from the fact that the loaves were divided and that there were baskets of food left over. The baskets of food might not have come from the original loaves. Symbolically, the original loaves might have inspired the spread of the "good news" far and wide.

This failure of the Gospels to be explicit about the multiplication of the loaves and fishes has also inspired another interpretation. Jesus was merely setting an example by dividing what he had among those near him. This made the others bring forth the food they had with them which they then shared with those around them. Hence, the baskets of scraps were from everyone's "picnic" and not from the remnants of the original loaves and fishes.

The general consensus of opinion about this miracle is that it is impossible at this late date to reconstruct what really happened. All we can do is to guess. The facts as set down in the Gospels seem to have so much omitted, and perhaps to have been exaggerated to such an extent (the 5000 or 4000 is, no doubt, an expanded figure) that we can only speculate. Do this, attempting to piece together a plausible account of the event which would fit the facts given, after taking account of heightening and exaggeration.

Another "nature" miracle is the one about "Jesus Walking on the Sea." This is found in Mark 6:45-52; Matthew 14:22-33; and John 6:16-21.

Mark 6:45-52

45 Immediately he made his disciples get into the boat and go before him to the other side, to Bethsaida, while he dismissed the crowd. [46] And after he had taken leave of them he went into the hills to pray. [47] And when evening came, the boat was out on the sea, and he was alone on the land. [48] And he saw that they were distressed in rowing, for the wind was against them. And about the fourth watch of the night he came to them, walking on the sea. He meant to pass by them, [49] but when they saw him walking on the sea, they thought it was a ghost, and cried out; [50] for they all saw him and were terrified. But immediately he spoke to them and said, "Take heart, it is I; have no fear."

[51] And he got into the boat with them and the wind ceased. And they were utterly astounded, [52] for they did not understand about the loaves, but their hearts were hardened.

Matthew 14:22-33

22 Then he made the disciples get into the boat and go before him to the other side, while he dismissed the crowds. [23] And after he had dismissed the crowds, he went up into the hills by himself to pray.

When evening came he was there alone, [24] but the boat by this time was many furlongs distant from the land, beaten by the waves; for the wind was against them. [25] And in the fourth watch of the night he came to them, walking on the sea. [26] But when the disciples saw him walking on the sea, they were terrified, saying, "It is a ghost!" And they cried out for fear. [27] But immediately he spoke to them, saying, "Take heart, it is I; have no fear."

28 And Peter answered him, "Lord, if it is you, bid me come to you on the water." [29] He said, "Come." So Peter got out of the boat and walked on the water and came to Jesus; [30] but when he saw the wind, he was afraid, and beginning to sink cried out, "Lord save me." [31] Jesus immediately reached out his hand and caught him, saying to him, "O man of little faith, why did you doubt?"
[32] And when they got into the boat, the wind ceased. [33] And those in the boat worshiped him, saying, "Truly you are the Son of God."

John 6:16-21

16 When evening came, his disciples went down to the sea, [17] got into a boat, and started across the sea to Caper'naum. It was now dark, and Jesus had not yet come to them. [18] The sea rose because a strong wind was blowing. [19] When they had rowed about three or four miles, they saw Jesus walking on the sea and drawing near to the boat. They were frightened, [20] but he said to them, "It is I; do not be afraid." [21] Then they were glad to take him into the boat and immediately the boat was at the land to which they were going.

Notice the heightening of the miraculous in John.
What do you think of Peter's attempt to do what Jesus had done?
Why do you suppose this was included in Matthew?
What is your evaluation of the miracle?
Do you think it happened as written? If it did not do you think there is any possible explanation for it?

If you think it did happen, what do you think was the
    point of it?

Another miracle of a similar kind is found in Mark 11:12-
14 and 20-23; as well as Matthew 21: 18-22. Read both of
these, and note the heightening of the miracle in Matthew.
We can ask the same questions about this "nature miracle"
that we have about the others.

What is the point of it?

Does it seem possible that Jesus would, if he could, do
    such a thing and why?

Is it something which could really have happened?

There is an interesting clue which may throw some light
on the problem of how to interpret these miracles. Read Luke
13:6-9. Can you give an interpretation of "The Cursing of
the Fig Tree" with the help of Luke?

The Transfiguration

The three Synoptic Gospels record two events which seem
to be a prelude to the final week in the life of Jesus, because
they tell of the awareness of the Disciples of his Messiahship
and his acceptance of the title. These two events are the confession of Peter and the transfiguration. Sometimes they are
considered separately, as though they had no connection one
with the other, or because the transfiguration seems to be a
later insertion put into the record by the Gospel writers or
their predecessors after the last week was over. However that
may be, the Gospel writers consider them together, and so
shall we.

Mark 8:27-30

27 And Jesus went on with his disciples, to the villages of Caesare'a
Philippi; and on the way he asked his disciples, "Who do men say that

I am?" [28] And they told him, "John the Baptist; and others say, Eli'jah; and others one of the prophets." [29] And he asked them, "But who do you say that I am?" Peter answered him, "You are the Christ." [30] And he charged them to tell no one about him.

Matthew 16:13-20

13 Now when Jesus came into the district of Caesare'a Philippi, he asked his disciples, "Who do men say that the Son of man is?" [14] And they said, "Some say John the Baptist, others say Eli'jah, and others Jeremiah or one of the prophets." [15] He said to them, "But who do you say that I am?" [16] Simon Peter replied, "You are the Christ, the Son of the living God." [17] And Jesus answered him, "Blessed are you, Simon Bar-Jona! For flesh and blood has not revealed this to you, but my Father who is in heaven. [18]And I tell you, you are Peter, and on this rock I will build my church, and the powers of death shall not prevail against it. [19] I will give you the keys of the kingdom of heaven, and whatever you bind on earth shall be bound in heaven, and whatever you loose on earth shall be loosed in heaven." [20] Then he strictly charged the disciples to tell no one that he was the Christ.

Luke 9:18-22

18 Now it happened that as he was praying alone the disciples were with him; and he asked them, "Who do the people say that I am?" [19] And they answered, "John the Baptist; but others say, Eli'jah; and others, that one of the old prophets has risen." [20] And he said to them, "But who do you say that I am?" And Peter answered, "The Christ of God." [21] But he charged and commanded them to tell this to no one, [22] saying, "The Son of man must suffer many things, and be rejected by the elders and chief priests and scribes, and be killed, and on the third day be raised."

Read each of these versions of Peter's confession carefully. Make a list of the differences which you find in comparing the three. It will help you evaluate this story if you will review the meaning and significance of the following: Son of Man, Christ, Elijah. Basing your answer on your own knowledge of the Gospel writers and on your own interpretation of Jesus analyze Jesus' answer to Peter's "confession." Having arrived at your own conclusion, figure out how someone else, reading these passages, could arrive at quite another conclusion. Leaving aside for the moment the question of whether Jesus thought of himself as the Messiah, what do these passages show concerning the popular conception of his role?

Read the story of the transfiguration and compare the versions.

Mark 9:2-13

2 And after six days Jesus took with him Peter and James and John, and led them up a high mountain apart by themselves; and he was transfigured before them, ³ and his garments became glistening, intensely white, as no fuller on earth could bleach them. ⁴ And there appeared to them Eli'jah with Moses: and they were talking to Jesus. ⁵ And Peter said to Jesus, "Master, it is well that we are here; let us make three booths, one for you and one for Moses and one for Eli'jah." ⁶ For he did not know what to say, for they were exceedingly afraid. ⁷ And a cloud overshadowed them, and a voice came out of the cloud, "This is my beloved Son; listen to him." ⁸ And suddenly looking around they no longer saw any one with them but Jesus only.

9 And as they were coming down the mountain, he charged them to tell no one what they had seen, until the Son of man should have risen from the dead. ¹⁰ So they kept the matter to themselves, questioning what the rising from the dead meant. ¹¹ And they asked him, "Why do the scribes say that first Eli'jah must come?" ¹² And he said to them, "Eli'jah does come first to restore all things; and how is it written of the Son of man, that he should suffer many things and be treated with contempt? ¹³ But I tell you that Eli'jah has come, and they did to him whatever they pleased, as it is written of him."

Matthew 17:1-13

1 And after six days Jesus took with him Peter and James and John his brother, and led them up a high mountain apart.

² And he was transfigured before them, and his face shone like the sun, and his garments became white as light. ³ And behold, there appeared to them Moses and Eli'jah, talking with him. ⁴ And Peter said to Jesus, "Lord, it is well that we are here; if you wish, I will make three booths here, one for you and one for Moses and one for Eli'jah." ⁵ He was still speaking, when lo, a bright cloud overshadowed them, and a voice from the cloud said, "This is my beloved Son, with whom I am well pleased; listen to him." ⁶ When the disciples heard this, they fell on their faces, and were filled with awe. ⁷ But Jesus came and touched them saying, "Rise, and have no fear." ⁸ And when they lifted up their eyes, they saw no one but Jesus only.

9 And as they were coming down the mountain, Jesus commanded them, "Tell no one the vision, until the Son of man is raised from the dead." [10] And the disciples asked him, "Then why do the scribes say that first Eli'jah must come?" [11] He replied, "Eli'jah does come, and he is to restore all things; [12] but I tell you that Eli'jah has already come, and they did not know him, but did to him whatever they pleased. So also the Son of man will suffer at their hands." [13] Then the disciples understood that he was speaking to them of John the Baptist.

Luke 9:28-36

28 Now about eight days after these sayings he took with him Peter and John and James, and went up on the mountain to pray. [29] And as he was praying, the appearance of his countenance was altered, and his raiment became dazzling white. [30] And behold, two men talked with him, Moses and Eli'jah, [31] who appeared in glory and spoke of his departure, which he was to accomplish at Jerusalem. [32] Now Peter and those who were with him were heavy with sleep but kept awake, and they saw his glory and the two men who stood with him. [33] And as the men were parting from him, Peter said to Jesus, "Master, it is well that we are here; let us make three booths, one for you and one for Moses and one for Eli'jah"—not knowing what he said. [34] As he said this, a cloud came and overshadowed them; and they were afraid as they entered the cloud. [35] And a voice came out of the cloud, saying, "This is my Son, my Chosen; listen to him!" [36] And when the voice had spoken, Jesus was found alone. And they kept silence and told no one in those days anything of what they had seen.

How would you interpret this event?

How did the Gospel writers interpret it?

If you have found difficulty in arriving at an interpretation which is satisfactory to you, it might be of some comfort to know that there is no agreement among scholars as to the "right" interpretation. This is one of the most difficult passages in the Gospels to understand, if by understanding we mean knowing what was the actual event behind the Gospel story, if there was such an event. Below are some interpretations which have been given to it. Which one seems most reasonable to you?

First, there is the literal interpretation that the story means just what it says. Jesus was changed into a glowing white figure, a voice from heaven was heard by the Disciples and Moses and Elijah were actually there.

Another possible interpretation is that this is actually a misplaced resurrection appearance. This theory places the episode at the end of the Gospels, along with the other post-crucifixion appearances. Those holding this view point out that the transfiguration is an episode similar to those later appearances, and that after the crucifixion many accepted Jesus as Messiah. Those who did not accept him as the Messiah needed to be convinced (one of the reasons the Gospels were written), hence the inclusion of Moses and Elijah to give validity to the assertion of the Messiahship of Jesus and the placing of this recognition before the crucifixion. The purpose of these passages, then, was to show that the Disciples recognized Jesus' Messiahship as early as this.

Still another interpretation is the symbolic one. All parts of the narrative need to be seen as symbols. The white garment symbolizes the other world; Moses and Elijah stand for the Law and the Prophets; the voice from heaven shows God's approval. The whole story symbolizes the acceptance of Jesus as Messiah by the Disciples, but is not to be taken literally.

Yet another interpretation would see in the transfiguration a personal experience of Jesus which made him aware of the fact that he was the Messiah, with all of its consequences for him personally. This personal experience has, with time, come to be taken as literal. This is, of course, the same interpretation which many have given to the baptism and temptation stories. This same kind of explanation could be given to the transfiguration as an experience, not of Jesus, but of the Disciples. While Jesus was away from them for a while, the three main Disciples suddenly realized that their leader was, in reality, the Messiah. As this experience was told and re-told, it became more and more literal until it attained the form it now has.

Others see in the transfiguration a story from the early

church. The followers of Jesus who carried on his work after his tragic death believed that Jesus was the Messiah. It was this belief which kept the early Christian movement alive. Such an explanation would make this incident one inserted into the record to show that as early as this some of the Disciples realized the true nature of Jesus; but because Jesus told them not to tell, others did not know it.

Almost everyone who has studied this event with care has concluded that, whatever one's interpretation, it is clear that from this time on the Disciples, or some of them at least, thought of Jesus as fulfilling a messianic role. Whether he thought of himself as filling that role is another question upon which there is no agreement.

If you have time, read another passage in the three Synoptics which is equally difficult to interpret, but which shows the dilemma of interpretation very well. This passage is found in Mark 8:31-9:1; Matthew 16:21-28; and Luke 9:22-27. Try your hand at giving it a variety of interpretations.

The Entry into Jerusalem

Between the story of the transfiguration and the story of the entry into Jerusalem, there are a number of accounts of the teaching of Jesus and of his healing ministry as he made his way toward the Holy City. The next important event in his life was the entry into Jerusalem.

Mark 11:1-10
And when they drew near to Jerusalem, to Beth'phage and Bethany, at the Mount of Olives, he sent two of his disciples, [2] and said to them, "Go into the village opposite you, and immediately as you enter it you will find a colt tied, on which no one has ever sat; untie it and bring it. [3] If any one says to you, 'Why are you doing this?' say, 'The Lord has

need of it and will send it back here immediately.' " [4] And they went away, and found a colt tied at the door out in the open street; and they untied it. [5] And those who stood there said to them, "What are you doing, untying the colt?" [6] And they told them what Jesus had said; and they let them go. [7] And they brought the colt to Jesus, and threw their garments on it; and he sat upon it. [8] And many spread their garments on the road, and others spread leafy branches which they had cut from the fields. [9] And those who went before and those who followed cried out, "Hosanna! Blessed is he who comes in the name of the Lord! [10] Blessed is the kingdom of our father David that is coming! Hosanna in the highest!"

Matthew 21:1-9

And when they drew near to Jerusalem and came to Beth'phage, to the Mount of Olives, then Jesus sent two disciples, [2] saying to them, "Go into the village opposite you, and immediately you will find an ass tied, and a colt with her; untie them and bring them to me. [3] If any one says anything to you, you shall say, 'The Lord has need of them,' and he will send them immediately." [4] This took place to fulfil what was spoken by the prophet, saying,

[5] "Tell the daughter of Zion,
Behold, your king is coming to you,
humble, and mounted on an ass,
and on a colt, the foal of an ass."

[6] The disciples went and did as Jesus had directed them; [7] they brought the ass and the colt, and put their garments on them, and he sat thereon. [8] Most of the crowd spread their garments on the road, and others cut branches from the trees and spread them on the road. [9] And the crowds that went before him and that followed him shouted, "Hosanna to the Son of David! Blessed is he who comes in the name of the Lord! Hosanna in the highest!"

Luke 19:29-38

[29] When he drew near to Beth'phage and Bethany, at the mount that is called Olivet, he sent two of the disciples, [30] saying, "Go into the village opposite, where on entering you will find a colt tied, on which no one has ever yet sat; untie it and bring it here. [31] If any one asks you, 'Why are you untying it?' you shall say this, 'The Lord has need of it.' " [32] So those who were sent went away and found it as he had told them. [33] And as they were untying the colt, its owners said to them, "Why are you untying the colt?" [34] And they said, "The Lord has need of it." [35] And they brought it to Jesus, and throwing their garments on the colt they set Jesus upon it. [36] And as he rode along, they spread

their garments on the road. [37] As he was now drawing near, at the descent of the Mount of Olives, the whole multitude of the disciples began to rejoice and praise God with a loud voice for all the mighty works that they had seen, [38] saying, "Blessed is the King who comes in the name of the Lord! Peace in heaven and glory in the highest!"

Compare the versions, and interpret what happened. Give another possible interpretation. Put the passage into your own words as though you were a news reporter "covering" the story. Make this account matter-of-fact, including all the details as, for example, how the Disciples managed to get a colt for Jesus to ride on. Read some Palm Sunday hymns in your own hymn book and see how they tell this story.

Following closely after the entry into Jerusalem, all three Gospels record the cleansing of the Temple. Can you reconcile this with the teaching in the Sermon on the Mount about "turning the other cheek"?

Mark 11:15-18

15 And they came to Jerusalem. And he entered the temple and began to drive out those who sold and those who bought in the temple, and he overturned the tables of the money-changers and the seats of those who sold pigeons; [16] and he would not allow any one to carry anything through the temple. [17] And he taught, and said to them, "Is it not written, 'My house shall be called a house of prayer for all the nations'? But you have made it a den of robbers." [18] And the chief priests and the scribes heard it and sought a way to destroy him; for they feared him, because all the multitude was astonished at his teaching.

Matthew 21:12-13

12 And Jesus entered the temple of God and drove out all who sold and bought in the temple, and he overturned the tables of the money-changers and the seats of those who sold pigeons. [13] He said to them, "It is written, 'My house shall be called a house of prayer'; but you make it a den of robbers."

Luke 19:45-46

45 And he entered the temple and began to drive out those who sold, [46] saying to them, "It is written, 'My house shall be a house of prayer'; but you have made it a den of robbers."

Included in this section are several examples of how the groups who disapproved of the teaching of Jesus attempted to trip him up. Look at Mark 11:27-33. The parallels in the other two Gospels add nothing to this. What do you think of Jesus' answer? Read Mark 12:13-17. Again the parallels add nothing. What do you think Jesus' answer means? Read Mark 12:18-27. Matthew is substantially the same, but Luke makes the passage a little easier to understand (Luke 20:27-40). Put into your own words the logical argument with which Jesus answers the Sadducees.

Another passage which both Mark and Matthew place in this same section, but which Luke places in another setting, is the passage about the greatest commandment. In a way this sums up the central point of all the teaching of Jesus. See if you agree with this statement, or if you would like to add something to the teaching as it is set forth here.

Mark 12:28-34

28 And one of the scribes came up and heard them disputing with one another, and seeing that he answered them well, asked him, "Which commandment is the first of all?" [29] Jesus answered, "The first is, 'Hear, O Israel: The Lord our God , the Lord is one; [30] and you shall love the Lord your God with all your heart, and with all your soul, and with all your mind, and with all your strength.' [31] The second is this, 'You shall love your neighbor as yourself.' There is no other commandment greater than these." [32] And the scribe said to him, "You are right, Teacher; you have truly said that he is one, and there is no other but he; [33] and to love him with all the heart, and with all the understanding, and with all the strength, and to love one's neighbor as oneself, is much more than all whole burnt offerings and sacrifices." [34] And when Jesus saw that he answered wisely, he said to him, "You are not far from the kingdom of God." And after that no one dared to ask him any question.

Matthew 22: 34-40

34 But when the Pharisees heard that he had silenced the Sad'ducees, they came together. [35] And one of them, a lawyer, asked him a question, to test him. [36] "Teacher, which is the great commandment in the law?" [37] And he said to him, "You shall love the Lord your God with all your heart, and with all your soul, and with all your mind. [38] This

is the great and first commandment. [39] And a second is like it, You shall love your neighbor as yourself. [40] On these two commandments depend all the law and the prophets."

Luke 10:25-28

25 And behold, a lawyer stood up to put him to the test, saying, "Teacher, what shall I do to inherit eternal life?" [26] He said to him, "What is written in the law? How do you read?" [27] And he answered, "You shall love the Lord your God with all your heart, and with all your soul, and with all your strength, and with all your mind; and your neighbor as yourself." [28] And he said to him, "You have answered right; do this, and you will live."

We have now arrived at the sequence of events which Christians call Holy Week. This week begins with Palm Sunday and terminates with Easter. The episodes recorded here are the best-known part of the entire life of Jesus. The devout have pored over these pages and meditated on these events for century upon century. Each year in great cathedrals and in the little parish churches all over the world this week is celebrated as the holiest week of the year. It begins in triumph with the entry into Jerusalem, it progresses through treachery to tragedy and culminates with great exaltation in Easter Sunday, the day of resurrection.

As we look at these events and attempt to discover what actual happenings lie behind them, we must never forget that the true importance of them lies not in what objectively happened, but in what people thought happened, what subjectively they felt about these events. It has been said that the Jesus of History is not nearly so important as the Christ of Faith. We are interested here in the Jesus of History, but we must keep before our eyes the important fact that it was the Christ of Faith who lived on in the hearts and minds of men. The Jesus of History is dimly seen, but the Christ of Faith is central in the religion of millions of Christians.

To appreciate the full sweep of the events of this momentous week, it would be well to read the story all the way through before we discuss the various parts. Since Mark is the earliest Gospel, his version is the logical one to read. Read Mark 14:10-16:8. Read it as you would a story, following the drama as it unfolds. Try not to be too critical of it. Imagine yourself in the first century reading the newly written Gospel of Mark which tells of the events about which you have heard so many rumors. Pretend that this is the first time you have ever read about this in one continuous narrative.

Now that we have read the whole, let us go back to look at the various episodes one by one, and discover what we can about the historical Jesus.

The Last Supper

The great importance of the Last Supper in Christianity lies in the fact that from it has come the Eucharist or Communion service. The development of this sacrament in the Christian church will form part of the discussion of the final chapter of this book.

Remember, however, that the use of the bread and the wine and the words which Jesus spoke on this occasion are central to that sacrament. We are interested here in the historical Jesus and so we wish to look at the event rather than at the significance which later practice and devotion gave it.

The date on which the Last Supper took place is disputed. There seems to be no way of being sure exactly when it took place. This is important, because if we knew the date of the Last Supper, we would be able to date the crucifixion and then work back to fix with reasonable certainty the other dates in the life of Jesus. However, there is no agreement. The Synoptic Gospels and John give different dates. The arguments for one date or another and the reasons for the uncertainty are very complicated. Suffice it to say that the date of A.D. 30 is the one most generally accepted, although it is recognized that this date may not be accurate.

The nature of the meal which is described is also a matter of dispute. The Gospels tell us that Jesus and his Disciples were celebrating the Passover. This would indicate that the meal they were having together was a Seder, or Passover meal, held the evening before. However, if this is accurate, then Jesus must have been crucified on Passover itself, an unlikely date to have been chosen for an execution since it was an important religious holiday.

It is possible that it was a Seder which Jesus celebrated ahead of time because he knew that his life was in danger. He may have realized that he would not be able to meet his Disciples on the next day because those looking for him would expect him to celebrate on that day. It is also possible that this was not a Seder meal at all, but was like those ritual meals which were celebrated by the Essene group which probably included only bread and wine. It is possible, too, that there was a dispute among the various sects of Judaism as to the exact date on which Passover was to be celebrated, so that in fact there may have been two celebrations.

It may also be that the story of this meal is written down in the Gospels as it was remembered. Jesus and his Disciples were too poor to have a more elaborate meal. In other words, the meal itself had no great significance except that it became the last one which the Disciples had with Jesus. This in itself would give it a special importance, if not a sacredness, which at the time it would not have had. As time went on, remembrance embellished it with special importance. It is interesting to note in this connection that the earliest Communion was the sacred meal, or love feast, which was celebrated in the early church. Paul tells about the abuse of it in I Corinthians 11:20-34. Take time and read about it.

In short, to arrive at any definite conclusion concerning the date, or the exact nature of this Last Supper, seems impossible at the present time. Reread this section in Mark 14:12-25. Reconstruct this as if you were there and explain what it was like. Before you do this read the versions of the other two Synoptics (Matthew 26:17-29; Luke 22:7-23) to get all the facts you can.

The Garden of Gethsemane

Read Mark 14:32-52, which follows.

32 And they went to a place which was called Gethsem'ane; and he said to his disciples. "Sit here while I pray." [33] And he took with him Peter and James and John, and began to be greatly distressed and troubled. [34] And he said to them, "My soul is very sorrowful, even to death; remain here, and watch." [35] And going a little farther, he fell on the ground and prayed that, if it were possible, the hour might pass from him. [36] And he said, "Abba, Father, all things are possible to thee; remove this cup from me; yet not what I will, but what thou wilt." [37] And he came and found them sleeping, and he said to Peter, "Simon, are you asleep? Could you not watch one hour? [38] Watch and pray that you may not enter into temptation; the spirit indeed is willing, but the flesh is weak." [39] And again he went away and prayed, saying the same words. [40] And again he came and found them sleeping, for their eyes were very heavy; and they did not know what to answer him. [41] And he came the third time, and said to them, "Are you still sleeping and taking your rest? It is enough; the hour has come; the Son of man is betrayed into the hands of sinners. [42] Rise, let us be going; see, my betrayer is at hand."

43 And immediately, while he was still speaking, Judas came, one of the twelve, and with him a crowd with swords and clubs, from the chief priests and the scribes and the elders. [44] Now the betrayer had given them a sign, saying, "The one I shall kiss is the man; seize him and lead him away safely." [45] And when he came, he went up to him at once, and said, "Master!" And he kissed him. [46] And they laid hands on him and seized him. [47] But one of those who stood by drew his sword, and struck the slave of the high priest and cut off his ear. [48] And Jesus said to them, "Have you come out as against a robber, with swords and clubs to capture me? [49] Day after day I was with you in the temple teaching, and you did not seize me. But let the scriptures be fulfilled." [50] And they all forsook him, and fled.

51 And a young man followed him, with nothing but a linen cloth

about his body; and they seized him, [52] but he left the linen cloth and ran away naked.

Try to explain these parts of the story:
What Jesus meant by his prayer.
The Disciples' realization of what was about to happen.
The phrase, "the kiss of Judas."
The purpose of verses 51-52.
Now read the parallel versions:

Matthew 26:30-56

30 And when they had sung a hymn, they went out to the Mount of Olives. [31] Then Jesus said to them, "You will all fall away because of me this night; for it is written, 'I will strike the shepherd, and the sheep of the flock will be scattered.' [32] But after I am raised up, I will go before you to Galilee." [33] Peter declared to him, "Though they all fall away because of you, I will never fall away." [34] Jesus said to him, "Truly, I say to you, this very night, before the cock crows, you will deny me three times." [35] Peter said to him, "Even if I must die with you, I will not deny you." And so said all the disciples.

36 Then Jesus went with them to a place called Gethsem'ane, and he said to his disciples, "Sit here, while I go yonder and pray." [37] And taking with him Peter and the two sons of Zeb'edee, he began to be sorrowful and troubled. [38] Then he said to them, "My soul is very sorrowful, even to death; remain here, and watch with me." [39] And going a little farther he fell on his face and prayed, "My Father, if it be possible, let this cup pass from me; nevertheless, not as I will, but as thou wilt." [40] And he came to the disciples and found them sleeping; and he said to Peter, "So, could you not watch with me one hour? [41] Watch and pray that you may not enter into temptation; the spirit indeed is willing, but the flesh is weak." [42] Again, for the second time, he went away and prayed, "My Father, if this cannot pass unless I drink it, thy will be done." [43] And again he came and found them sleeping, for their eyes were heavy. [44] So, leaving them again, he went away and prayed for the third time, saying the same words. [45] Then he came to the disciples and said to them, "Are you still sleeping and taking your rest? Behold, the hour is at hand, and the Son of man is betrayed into the hands of sinners. [46] Rise, let us be going; see, my betrayer is at hand."

47 While he was still speaking, Judas came, one of the twelve, and with him a great crowd with swords and clubs, from the chief priests and the elders of the people. [48] Now the betrayer had given them a sign,

saying, "The one I shall kiss is the man; seize him." [49] And he came up to Jesus at once and said, "Hail, Master!" And he kissed him. [50] Jesus said to him, "Friend, why are you here?" Then they came up and laid hands on Jesus and seized him. [51] And behold, one of those who were with Jesus stretched out his hand and drew his sword, and struck the slave of the high priest, and cut off his ear. [52] Then Jesus said to him, "Put your sword back into its place; for all who take the sword will perish by the sword. [53] Do you think that I cannot appeal to my Father, and he will at once send me more than twelve legions of angels? [54] But how then should the scriptures be fulfilled, that it must be so?" [55] At that hour Jesus said to the crowds, "Have you come out as against a robber, with swords and clubs to capture me? Day after day I sat in the temple teaching, and you did not seize me. [56] But all this has taken place, that the scriptures of the prophets might be fulfilled." Then all the disciples forsook him and fled.

Luke 22:40-53

[40] And when he came to the place he said to them, "Pray that you may not enter into temptation." [41] And he withdrew from them about a stone's throw, and knelt down and prayed, [42] "Father, if thou art willing, remove this cup from me; nevertheless not my will, but thine, be done." [43] And there appeared to him an angel from heaven, strengthening him. [44] And being in an agony he prayed more earnestly; and his sweat became like great drops of blood falling down upon the ground.[1] [45] And when he rose from prayer, he came to the disciples and found them sleeping for sorrow, [46] and he said to them, "Why do you sleep? Rise and pray that you may not enter into temptation."

47 While he was still speaking, there came a crowd, and the man called Judas, one of the twelve, was leading them. He drew near to Jesus to kiss him; [48] but Jesus said to him, "Judas, would you betray the Son of man with a kiss?" [49] And when those who were about him saw what would follow, they said, "Lord, shall we strike with the sword?" [50] And one of them struck the slave of the high priest and cut off his right ear. [51] But Jesus said, "No more of this!" And he touched his ear and healed him. [52] Then Jesus said to the chief priests and captains of the temple and elders, who had come out against him, "Have you come out as against a robber, with swords and clubs? [53] When I was with you day after day in the temple, you did not lay hands on me. But this is your hour, and the power of darkness."

Compare each of these with Mark's version, stating in each case where you find a difference the reason you think

Matthew or Luke differed at that point. Which Gospel do you think is the most reliable? Give your reasons for your choice.

Peter's Denial

Explain as best you can, Peter's behavior from the time of the Last Supper to the crucifixion. Try to give reasons for his failing to keep watch in the garden and for his denial.

Trial Before the Sanhedrin

Reread Mark 14:53-65. What impression does Mark leave with respect to the trial? Does he imply that it was a fair trial? What did the "false witnesses" say about Jesus according to Mark? Read Mark 13:1-2. What did Jesus say in answer to the question about himself? On what grounds did the Sanhedrin convict him?

Read Matthew 26:57-68. Answer the same questions about this passage that you did about Mark. Do the same with Luke 22:54-71.

Trial Before Pilate

Read the three versions of this story.

Mark 15:1-15
And as soon as it was morning the chief priests, with the elders and

144

scribes, and the whole council held a consultation; and they bound Jesus and led him away and delivered him to Pilate. ² And Pilate asked him, "Are you the King of the Jews?" And he answered him. "You have said so." ³ And the chief priests accused him of many things. ⁴ And Pilate again asked him,"Have you no answer to make? See how many charges they bring against you." ⁵ But Jesus made no further answer, so that Pilate wondered.

6 Now at the feast he used to release for them one prisoner whom they asked. ⁷ And among the rebels in prison, who had committed murder in the insurrection, there was a man called Barab'bas. ⁸ And the crowd came up and began to ask Pilate to do as he was wont to do for them. ⁹ And he answered them, "Do you want me to release for you the King of the Jews?" ¹⁰ For he perceived that it was out of envy that the chief priests had delivered him up. ¹¹ But the chief priests stirred up the crowd to have him release for them Barab'bas instead. ¹² And Pilate again said to them, "Then what shall I do with the man whom you call the King of the Jews?" ¹³ And they cried out again, "Crucify him." ¹⁴ And Pilate said to them, "Why, what evil has he done?" But they shouted all the more, "Crucify him." ¹⁵ So Pilate, wishing to satisfy the crowd, released for them Barab'bas; and having scourged Jesus, he delivered him to be crucified.

Matthew 27:1-26

When morning came, all the chief priests and the elders of the people took counsel against Jesus to put him to death; ² and they bound him and led him away and delivered him to Pilate the governor.

3 When Judas, his betrayer, saw that he was condemned, he repented and brought back the thirty pieces of silver to the chief priests and the elders, ⁴ saying, "I have sinned in betraying innocent blood." They said, "What is that to us? See to it yourself." ⁵ And throwing down the pieces of silver in the temple, he departed; and he went and hanged himself. ⁶ But the chief priests, taking the pieces of silver, said, "It is not lawful to put them into the treasury, since they are blood money." ⁷ So they took council, and bought with them the potter's field, to bury strangers in. ⁸ Therefore that field has been called the Field of Blood to this day. ⁹ Then was fulfilled what had been spoken by the prophet Jeremiah, saying, "And they took the thirty pieces of silver, the price of him on whom a price has been set by some of the sons of Israel, ¹⁰ and they gave them for the potter's field, as the Lord directed me."

11 Now Jesus stood before the governor; and the governor asked him, "Are you the King of the Jews?" Jesus said to him, "You have

said so." 12 But when he was accused by the chief priests and elders, he made no answer. 13 Then Pilate said to him, "Do you not hear how many things they testify against you?" 14 But he gave him no answer, not even to a single charge; so the governor wondered greatly.

15 Now at the feast the governor was accustomed to release for the crowd any one prisoner whom they wanted. 16 And they had then a notorious prisoner called Barab'bas. 17 So when they had gathered, Pilate said to them, "Whom do you want me to release for you, Barab'bas or Jesus who is called Christ?" 18 For he knew that it was out of envy that they had delivered him up. 19 Besides, while he was sitting on the judgment seat, his wife sent word to him, "Have nothing to do with that righteous man, for I have suffered much over him, today in a dream." 20 Now the chief priests and the elders persuaded the people to ask for Barab'bas and destroy Jesus. 21 The governor again said to them, "Which of the two do you want me to release for you?" And they said, "Barab'bas." 22 Pilate said to them, "Then what shall I do with Jesus who is called Christ?" They all said, "Let him be crucified." 23 And he said, "Why, what evil has he done?" But they shouted all the more, "Let him be crucified."

24 So when Pilate saw that he was gaining nothing, but rather that a riot was beginning, he took water and washed his hands before the crowd, saying, "I am innocent of this man's blood; see to it yourselves." 25 And all the people answered, "His blood be on us and on our children!" 26 Then he released for them Barab'bas, and having scourged Jesus, delivered him to be crucified.

Luke 23:1-25

Then the whole company of them arose, and brought him before Pilate. 2 And they began to accuse him, saying, "We found this man perverting our nation, and forbidding us to give tribute to Caesar, and saying that he himself is Christ a king." 3 And Pilate asked him, "Are you the King of the Jews?" And he answered him, "You have said so." 4 And Pilate said to the chief priests and the multitudes, "I find no crime in this man." 5 But they were urgent, saying, "He stirs up the people, teaching throughout all Judea, from Galilee even to this place."

6 When Pilate heard this, he asked whether the man was a Galilean. 7 And when he learned that he belonged to Herod's jurisdiction, he sent him over to Herod, who was himself in Jerusalem at that time. 8 When Herod saw Jesus, he was very glad, for he had long desired to see him, and he was hoping to see some sign done by him. 9 So he questioned him at some length; but he made no answer. 10 The chief priests and the scribes stood by, vehemently accusing him. 11 And Herod with his

soldiers treated him with contempt and mocked him; then, arraying him in gorgeous apparel, he sent him back to Pilate. [12] And Herod and Pilate became friends with each other that very day, for before this they had been at enmity with each other.

13 Pilate then called together the chief priests and the rulers and the people, [14] and said to them, "You brought me this man as one who was perverting the people; and after examining him before you, behold, I did not find this man guilty of any of your charges against him; [15] neither did Herod, for he sent him back to us. Behold, nothing deserving death has been done by him; [16] I will therefore chastise him and release him."

19 But they all cried out together, "Away with this man, and release to us Barab'bas"—[19] a man who had been thrown into prison for an insurrection started in the city, and for murder. [20] Pilate addressed them once more, desiring to release Jesus; [21] but they shouted out, "Crucify, crucify him!" [22] A third time he said to them, "Why, what evil has he done? I have found in him no crime deserving death; I will therefore chastise him and release him." [23] But they were urgent, demanding with loud cries that he should be crucified. And their voices prevailed. [24] So Pilate gave sentence that their demand should be granted. [25] He released the man who had been thrown into prison for insurrection and murder, whom they asked for; but Jesus he delivered up to their will.

What answer did Jesus give about himself in the three Gospels?

Whom do the Gospel writers blame for the death of Jesus?

Do you detect any difference in emphasis on this point in any of them?

If so, can you give a reason for it?

According to the Gospels, who actually gave the order for the crucifixion?

What reasons, aside from those given in the Gospels, do you think he had for putting Jesus to death?

Pretend that you are Pontius Pilate writing a report to the Emperor on the crucifixion of Jesus. What would you say? If you were a member of the Sanhedrin writing up the events of the day, what would you have to say about the trial of Jesus?

What would you have written if you were Peter writing in his diary—presuming he could write and had a diary? Summarize what the Gospel writer did write some 40 to 60 years later.

The Crucifixion

Read all three accounts of the crucifixion.

Mark 15:16-41

16 And the soldiers led him away inside the palace (that is, the praetorium); and they called together the whole battalion. [17] And they clothed him in a purple cloak, and plaiting a crown of thorns they put it on him. [18] And they began to salute him, "Hail, King of the Jews!" [19] And they struck his head with a reed, and spat upon him, and they knelt down in homage to him. [20] And when they had mocked him, they stripped him of the purple cloak, and put his own clothes on him. And they led him out to crucify him.

21 And they compelled a passer-by, Simon of Cyre'ne, who was coming in from the country, the father of Alexander and Rufus, to carry his cross. [22] And they brought him to the place called Gol'gotha (which means the place of a skull). [23] And they offered him wine mingled with myrrh; but he did not take it. [24] And they crucified him, and divided his garments among them, casting lots for them, to decide what each should take. [25] And it was the third hour, when they crucified him. [26] And the inscription of the charge against him read, "The King of the Jews" [27] And with him they crucified two robbers, one on his right and one on his left. [29] And those who passed by derided him, wagging their heads, and saying, "Aha! You who would destroy the temple and build it in three days, [30] save yourself and come down from the cross!" [31] So also the chief priests mocked him to one another with the scribes, saying, "He saved others; he cannot save himself. [32] Let the Christ, the King of Israel, come down now from the cross, that we may see and believe." Those who were crucified with him also reviled him.

33 And when the sixth hour had come, there was darkness over the whole land until the ninth hour. [34] And at the ninth hour Jesus cried with a loud voice, "E'lo-i, E'lo-i, la'ma sabach-tha'ni?" which means,

"My God, my God, why hast thou forsaken me?" [35] And some of the bystanders hearing it said, "Behold, he is calling Eli'jah." [36] And one ran and, filling a sponge full of vinegar, put it on a reed and gave it to him to drink, saying, "Wait, let us see whether Eli'jah will come to take him down." [37] And Jesus uttered a loud cry, and breathed his last. [38] And the curtain of the temple was torn in two, from top to bottom. [39] And when the centurion, who stood facing him, saw that he thus breathed his last, he said, "Truly this man was the Son of God!"

40 There were also women looking on from afar, among whom were Mary Mag'dalene, and Mary the mother of James the younger and of Joses, and Salo'me, [41] who, when he was in Galilee, followed him, and ministered to him; and also many other women who came up with him to Jerusalem.

Matthew 27:27-56

27 Then the soldiers of the governor took Jesus into the praetorium, and they gathered the whole battalion before him. [28] And they stripped him and put a scarlet robe upon him, [29] and plaiting a crown of thorns they put it on his head, and put a reed in his right hand. And kneeling before him they mocked him, saying, "Hail, King of the Jews!" [30] And they spat upon him, and took the reed and struck him on the head. [31] And when they had mocked him, they stripped him of the robe, and put his own clothes on him, and led him away to crucify him.

32 As they were marching out, they came upon a man of Cyre'ne, Simon by name; this man they compelled to carry his cross. [33] And when they came to a place called Gol'gotha (which means the place of a skull), [34] they offered him wine to drink, mingled with gall; but when he tasted it, he would not drink it. [35] And when they had crucified him, they divided his garments among them by casting lots; [36] then they sat down and kept watch over him there. [37] And over his head they put the charge against him, which read, "This is Jesus the King of the Jews." [38] Then two robbers were crucified with him, one on the right and one on the left. [39] And those who passed by derided him, wagging their heads [40]and saying, "You who would destroy the temple and build in three days, save yourself! If you are the Son of God, come down from the cross." [41] So also the chief priests, with the scribes and elders, mocked him, saying, [42] "He saved others; he cannot save himself. He is the King of Israel; let him come down now from the cross, and we will believe in him. [43] He trusts in God; let God deliver him now, if he desires him; for he said, 'I am the Son of God.' " [44] And the robbers who were crucified with him also reviled him in the same way.

45 Now from the sixth hour there was darkness over all the land

until the ninth hour. [46] And about the ninth hour Jesus cried with a loud voice, "Eli, Eli, la'ma sabach-tha'ni?" that is, "My God, my God, why hast thou forsaken me?" [47] And some of the bystanders hearing it said, "This man is calling Eli'jah." [48] And one of them at once ran and took a sponge, filled it with vinegar, and put it on a reed, and gave it to him to drink. [49] But the others said, "Wait, let us see whether Eli'jah will come to save him." [50] And Jesus cried again with a loud voice and yielded up his spirit.

51 And behold, the curtain of the temple was torn in two, from top to bottom; and the earth shook, and the rocks were split; [52] the tombs also were opened, and many bodies of the saints who had fallen asleep were raised, [53] and coming out of the tombs after his resurrection they went into the holy city and appeared to many. [54] When the centurion and those who were with him, keeping watch over Jesus, saw the earthquake and what took place, they were filled with awe, and said, "Truly this was the Son of God!"

55 There were also many women there, looking on from afar, who had followed Jesus from Galilee, ministering to him; [56] among whom were Mary Mag'dalene, and Mary the mother of James and Joseph, and the mother of the sons of Zeb'edee.

Luke 23:26-49

26 And as they led him away, they seized one Simon of Cyre'ne, who was coming in from the country, and laid on him the cross, to carry it behind Jesus. [27] And there followed him a great multitude of the people, and of women who bewailed and lamented him. [28] But Jesus turning to them said, "Daughters of Jerusalem, do not weep for me, but weep for yourselves and for your children. [29] For behold, the days are coming when they will say, 'Blessed are the barren, and the wombs that never bore, and the breasts that never gave suck!' [30] Then they will begin to say to the mountains, 'Fall on us'; and to the hills, 'Cover us.' [31] For if they do this when the wood is green, what will happen when it is dry?"

32 Two others also, who were criminals, were led away to be put to death with him. [33] And when they came to the place which is called The Skull, there they crucified him, and the criminals, one on the right, and one on the left. [34] And Jesus said, "Father, forgive them; for they know not what they do." And they cast lots to divide his garments. [35] And the people stood by, watching; but the rulers scoffed at him, saying, "He saved others; let him save himself, if he is the Christ of God, his Chosen One!" [36] The soldiers also mocked him, coming up and offering

him vinegar, [37] and saying, "If you are the King of the Jews, save yourself!" [38] There was also an inscription over him, "This is the King of the Jews."

39 One of the criminals who were hanged railed at him, saying, "Are you not the Christ? Save yourself and us!" [40] But the other rebuked him, saying, "Do you not fear God, since you are under the same sentence of condemnation? [41] And we indeed justly; for we are receiving the due reward of our deeds; but this man has done nothing wrong." [42] And he said, "Jesus, remember me when you come in your kingly power." [43] And he said to him, "Truly, I say to you, today you will be with me in Paradise."

44 It was now about the sixth hour, and there was darkness over the whole land until the ninth hour, [45] while the sun's light failed, and the curtain of the temple was torn in two. [46] Then Jesus, crying with a loud voice, said, "Father, into thy hands I commit my spirit!" And having said this he breathed his last. [47] Now when the centurion saw what had taken place, he praised God, and said, "Certainly this man was innocent!" [48] And all the multitudes who assembled to see the sight, when they saw what had taken place, returned home beating their breasts. [49] And all his acquaintances and the women who had followed him from Galilee stood at a distance and saw these things.

The details of the crucifixion as they are often depicted in Good Friday music, or in paintings, are taken from all three Gospels and combined as is customary, too, with the Christmas story. The events with which we are familiar are not all in one Gospel. In reading these accounts there are some things to remember: crucifixion was a common method of execution at this time. It was not a cruel invention made just for the purpose of torturing Jesus. The vinegar and gall which are mentioned were probably a drugged wine which was intended to dull the senses and help quench thirst. The curtain of the Temple was the curtain over the inner, most sacred spot. The symbolism here is that at the moment of the death of Jesus, Judaism was split asunder.

By now you should have learned enough about the kind of questions which can be raised to pose some questions for yourself, and see if you can find the answers.

Michelangelo (Italian, 1475 – 1564), La Pietà
A. Devaney, Inc., New York

Burial and Resurrection

Mark 15:42-16:8

42 And when evening had come, since it was the day of Preparation, that is, the day before the sabbath, ⁴³ Joseph of Arimathe'a, a respected member of the council, who was also himself looking for the kingdom of God, took courage and went to Pilate, and asked for the body of Jesus. ⁴⁴ And Pilate wondered if he were already dead; and summoning the centurion, he asked him whether he was already dead. ⁴⁵ And when he learned from the centurion that he was dead, he granted the body to Joseph. ⁴⁶ And he brought a linen shroud, and taking him down, wrapped him in the linen shroud, and laid him in a tomb which had been hewn out of the rock; and he rolled a stone against the door of the tomb. ⁴⁷ Mary Mag'dalene and Mary the mother of Joses saw where he was laid.

1 And when the sabbath was past, Mary Mag'dalene, and Mary the mother of James, and Salo'me, bought spices, so that they might go and anoint him. ² And very early on the first day of the week they went to the tomb when the sun had risen. ³ And they were saying to one another, "Who will roll away the stone for us from the door of the tomb?" ⁴ And looking up, they saw that the stone was rolled back for it was very large. ⁵ And entering the tomb, they saw a young man sitting on the right side, dressed in a white robe; and they were amazed. ⁶ And he said to them, "Do not be amazed; you seek Jesus of Nazareth, who was crucified. He has risen, he is not here; see the place where they laid him. ⁷ But go, tell his disciples and Peter that he is going before you to Galilee; there you will see him, as he told you." ⁸ And they went out and fled from the tomb; for trembling and astonishment had come upon them; and they said nothing to any one, for they were afraid.

Matthew 27:57-28:15

57 When it was evening, there came a rich man from Arimathe'a, named Joseph, who also was a disciple of Jesus. ⁵⁸ He went to Pilate and asked for the body of Jesus. Then Pilate ordered it to be given to him. ⁵⁹ And Joseph took the body, and wrapped it in a clean linen shroud, ⁶⁰ and laid it in his own new tomb, which he had hewn in the rock; and he rolled a great stone to the door of the tomb, and departed. ⁶¹ Mary Mag'dalene and the other Mary were there, sitting opposite the sepulchre.

62 Next day, that is, after the day of Preparation, the chief priests and the Pharisees gathered before Pilate [63] and said, "Sir, we remember how that imposter said, while he was still alive, 'After three days I will rise again.' [64] Therefore order the sepulchre to be made secure until the third day, lest his disciples go and steal him away, and tell the people, 'He has risen from the dead,' and the last fraud will be worse than the first." [65] Pilate said to them, "You have a guard of soldiers; go, make it as secure as you can." [66] So they went and made the sepulcher secure by sealing the stone and setting a guard.

1 Now after the sabbath, toward the dawn of the first day of the week Mary Mag'dalene and the other Mary went to see the sepulchre. [2]And behold, there was a great earthquake; for an angel of the Lord descended from heaven and came and rolled back the stone, and sat upon it. [3] His appearance was like lightning, and his raiment white as snow. [4] And for fear of him the guards trembled and became like dead men. [5] But the angel said to the women, "Do not be afraid; for I know that you seek Jesus who was crucified. [6] He is not here; for he has risen, as he said. Come, see the place where he lay. [7] Then go quickly and tell the disciples that he has risen from the dead, and behold, he is going before you to Galilee; there you will see him. Lo, I have told you." [8] So they departed quickly from the tomb with fear and great joy, and ran to tell his disciples. [9] And behold, Jesus met them and said, "Hail!" And they came up and took hold of his feet and worshiped him. [10] Then Jesus said to them, "Do not be afraid, go and tell my brethren to go to Galilee, and there they will see me."

11 While they were going, behold, some of the guard went into the city and told the chief priests all that had taken place. [12] And when they had assembled with the elders and taken counsel, they gave a sum of money to the soldiers [13] and said, "Tell people, 'His disciples came by night and stole him away while we were asleep.' [14] And if this comes to the governor's ears, we will satisfy him and keep you out of trouble." [15] So they took the money and did as they were directed; and this story has been spread among the Jews to this day.

Luke 23:50-24:11

50 Now there was a man named Joseph from the Jewish town of Arimathe'a. He was a member of the council, a good and righteous man, [51] who had not consented to their purpose and deed, and he was looking for the kingdom of God. [52] This man went to Pilate and asked for the body of Jesus. [53] Then he took it down and wrapped it in a linen shroud, and laid him in a rock-hewn tomb, where no one had ever yet been laid. [54] It was the day of Preparation, and the sabbath was be-

ginning. [55] The women who had come with him from Galilee followed, and saw the tomb, and how his body was laid; [56] then they returned, and prepared spices and ointments.

On the sabbath they rested according to the commandment.

[1] But on the first day of the week, at early dawn, they went to the tomb, taking the spices which they had prepared. [2] And they found the stone rolled away from the tomb, [3] but when they went in they did not find the body. [4] While they were perplexed about this, behold, two men stood by them in dazzling apparel; [5] and as they were frightened and bowed their faces to the ground, the men said to them, "Why do you seek the living among the dead? [6] Remember how he told you, while he was still in Galilee, [7] that the Son of man must be delivered into the hands of sinful men, and be crucified, and on the third day rise." [8] And they remembered his words, [9] and returning from the tomb they told all this to the eleven and to all the rest. [10] Now it was Mary Mag'dalene and Jo-an'na and Mary the mother of James and the other women with them who told this to the apostles; [11] but these words seemed to them an idle tale, and they did not believe them.

Before you discuss this section review your thinking about miracles.

How well do the three versions agree as to what happened?

Who discovered the empty tomb?

Who told them of the resurrection?

There are hints in the Gospels that there were those at the time who doubted that Jesus had risen from the dead and who gave their own explanation for it. To find out about this read Mark 15:44 and Matthew 28:11-15.

Resurrection Appearances

Note that the Gospel of Mark has an addition to it which most authorities think was added later. Whether the Gospel originally contained some resurrection appearances is not known. The Gospel seems to break off very abruptly, so perhaps it did. Read Matthew 28:9-10 and 16-20 as well as Luke 24:13-53.

How many explanations can you think of for these resurrection appearances? Which is the most acceptable to you?

Now that you have finished your study of Jesus, look at Chapter Two of this book again, and see if you would accept any of the interpretations of Jesus presented there. While you are studying them, ask yourself why you would reject or accept each one. Base your answers on the evidence in the New Testament.

It is interesting to compare the portrayals of Jesus which different people draw, and to see how they imagine the unknown years of Jesus' life, and how they interpret what he taught and how he thought of himself. The following are interesting, and will give you some contrast, although they are not extreme interpretations.

FAHS, SOPHIA L. *Jesus the Carpenter's Son*. Boston, Beacon, 1945.
FOSDICK, HARRY E. *Jesus of Nazareth*. New York, Random House, 1959.
GOODSPEED, EDGAR J. *A Life of Jesus*. New York, Harper, 1950. (Available in paperback: Harper Torch Books, TB 1)

We turn now to see what happened to the figure of Jesus after his death.

Chapter Eight: After the Crucifixion

One Creed, Differing Beliefs

Have you ever been to a church not your own? Was the service completely strange to you, or did you find parts which were familiar? You may have recognized the creed, or *credo*, meaning "I believe," which is repeated in many Christian churches, Protestant and Roman Catholic. Sometimes the creed recited is the Nicene, and sometimes it is the Apostles'. Here are the familiar words of the Nicene Creed, as they appear in *The Book of Common Prayer*, used in the Episcopal Church.

I believe in one God the Father Almighty, Maker of heaven and earth, and of all things visible and invisible:

And in one Lord Jesus Christ, the only begotten Son of God; Begotten of his Father before all worlds, God of God, Light of Light, Very God of very God; Begotten, not made; Being of one substance with the Father; By whom all things were made: Who for us men and for our salvation came down from heaven, And was incarnate by the Holy Ghost of the Virgin Mary, And was made man: And was crucified also for us under Pontius Pilate; He suffered and was buried: And the third day he rose again according to the Scriptures; And ascended into heaven, And sitteth on the right hand of the Father: And he shall come again, with glory, to judge both the quick and the dead; Whose kingdom shall have no end.

And I believe in the Holy Ghost, The Lord, and Giver of Life, Who proceedeth from the Father and the Son; Who with the Father and the Son together is worshipped and glorified; Who spake by the Prophets;

And I believe one Catholic and Apostolic Church: I acknowledge one Baptism for the remission of sins; And I look for the Resurrection of the dead: And the Life of the world to come. Amen.

How is it that these churches can include the same creeds in their services and yet have beliefs which are different? Why is it that some churches have no creed at all? What do the creeds mean? Is the Jesus of the creeds the same as the Jesus we have come to know? Make a list of questions about this creed which you would like to have answered. When the list is done, it is certain that the questions in it will not be easy to answer. Why is this?

Basic Attitudes

It is possible that some of the difficulty lies in differences in attitudes between the orthodox or traditional Christian and the liberal which makes it hard for them to understand each other. Those brought up in the liberal church tend to push aside any attempt to understand an idea such as the "Trinity" for example, as being irrelevant to them and the church and too obscure to merit the effort.

On the other hand, the answer of the traditional Christian to a question about belief is frequently based on the assumption that a person must start by having faith before understanding will come. This attitude creates a problem for those who insist on the use of reason in the search for religious answers and they will likely find this no answer at all. Faith, to such people, comes only after careful searching and deep thought. It does not "just happen." To base understanding on faith is, therefore, fruitless for them. Is this belief in the use of reason in religious matters a partial answer to why there is a problem in the meeting of minds between the groups? Is this difference important in attempting to understand the creeds?

As we look at the development of Christianity from the first century to the present, we find that there is another assumption upon which many leading Christian thinkers based their faith. This, too, has caused difficulties for those who could not accept it. The assumption was that man is inherently and hopelessly evil, and only if he receives help from God will he be able to achieve salvation. This theory holds that man can accomplish nothing himself. Salvation is construed as a future event, not of this world nor of this life, but entirely other-worldly and divinely given. The result of such a theory was to set men's eyes on the future life and to make of this life merely a preparation for the hereafter.

We cannot, of course, define too sharply, saying that all on this side of our definition are "liberal" and all on the other side are "orthodox." However, in attempting to understand the development of ideas concerning the nature of Christ we must bear in mind that for some these ideas rest on assumptions which are invalid, an approach to religious truth which is not acceptable. Neither point of view can be proved to be right. They are both, in a sense, resting on faith: the one on faith in man and his reason, the other on faith in God and the necessity for his help to miserable men. In turning now to consider Jesus as the generations after him came to look at him, we must remember these underlying differences in approach.

Jesus Becomes the Risen Christ

How is it that Jesus of Nazareth became the risen Christ? As we have seen, there are many indications that such a belief was held at the time that the Gospels were written. It is obvious that the authors of the Gospels thought of Jesus as the long-awaited Messiah. They believed that he was coming again, having overcome death and arisen from the tomb. That the Disciples did not hold this belief at first is probable. They were attracted to the preaching and the teaching of Jesus, feeling that in following him they would find the answer to their salvation. Some of them may have hoped that he might prove to be the kind of Messiah who would save their nation from the Roman oppression, and some of them may have looked upon him as the religious Messiah. The hopes of all were dashed with the arrest and crucifixion of their leader. How could a man who was executed as a common criminal be the savior of his people? If he could not save himself, how he possibly save others? As the Disciples pondered these questions, the feeling of Jesus' continuing influence and presence became strong. They began to be convinced that he would come back, that God would send him to usher in the Messianic Age.

Paul, too, as we have seen, had an other-worldly emphasis just as did the Disciples. Paul emphasized even more the complete helplessness of man to influence his own destiny.

[18] For I know that nothing good dwells within me, that is, in my flesh. I can will what is right, but I cannot do it. [19] For I do not do the good I want, but the evil I do not want is what I do. [20] Now if I do what I do not want, it is no longer I that do it, but sin which dwells within me.

Romans 7:18-20

Paul's concept of the nature of Jesus was somewhat different from that of the Disciples. He had been wrestling with the problem of religion for many years. He was a better educated man with a wider experience than the Disciples and his ideas were, understandably, more complicated. In the simplest terms, Paul thought of Jesus as having been in heaven from all eternity. When he came to earth he "emptied himself" of all his heavenly powers to become a man like us. After his earthly life he returned to heaven where he assumed all of his authority once again. He overcame death as an example to us. Those who believe in him will also achieve everlasting life. In Paul's own words:

> [5] Have this mind among yourselves, which you have in Christ Jesus, [6] who, though he was in the form of God, did not count equality with God a thing to be grasped, [7] but emptied himself, taking the form of a servant, being born in the likeness of men. [8] And being found in human form he humbled himself and became obedient unto death, even death on a cross. [9] Therefore God has highly exalted him and bestowed on him the name which is above every name, [10] that at the name of Jesus every knee should bow, in heaven and on earth and under the earth, [11] and every tongue confess that Jesus Christ is Lord, to the glory of God the Father.
>
> Philippians 2:5-11

The Last Supper Becomes Communion

Along with these ideas of what Jesus, the Christ, was like, went a development of ceremonies which helped the believer in his faith. One of the most important of these ceremonies was that of the Last Supper. We shall include it here because it will help us in our attempt to understand the beliefs about the nature of Christ which came to be held.

We have already considered the Last Supper as it is portrayed in the Gospels. We have also mentioned the way it was celebrated in the time of Paul. In this period, the Last Supper seems to have been a memorial, celebrated "in memory of me" as Jesus had instructed. The function of the feast in the early church at the time of Paul and shortly thereafter was also to give the Christians an opportunity for fellowship, much as our church suppers do today. In addition there was a ceremony of breaking the bread and of drinking the wine which was derived from the Last Supper which Jesus ate with his Disciples and which had a solemn religious meaning for the Christians.

Paul, and probably many of his contemporaries, took the Christian message of the risen Savior out into the Gentile world where the hope for salvation which it offered was accepted by many. In doing so, Paul interpreted Jesus and the meaning of his life in terms which could be readily understood by his listeners, as we have had occasion to note. The listeners, too, placed their own interpretation on the idea of "the supernatural become man and returned to heaven." In the Roman and Greek world the idea of a man-god was not uncommon. Look at all the myths about gods and mortals who married and had children who were half divine, half human. Jesus sounded like such a one to them. The idea of a dying and rising god was not an unfamiliar one, either. The mystery religions all revolved around such an idea, although in none of them was the hero known to be a historical man. The fact that Jesus had actually lived had great appeal. He was human, and somehow had achieved divinity. Man, too, wanted to accomplish this. The Last Supper became a ritual meal, more like that of the mystery religions than the Jewish Passover or the Essene banquet. A magical emphasis began to creep in. The idea arose that if one ate the bread and drank the wine he was actually eating the body and drinking the blood of the Savior. By so doing, according to this ancient belief, he would share in the Savior's divinity.

These developments led to an attempt on the part of the leaders of the Christian church to clarify some of the ideas involved. The first problem to be solved was to think through the relationship of Jesus and God. Was Jesus God? If he wasn't God, then where did he get his power to save people? If he were only a man, why worship him? Some thought this new religion was blasphemous, and many changes were brought against the Christians in this period because of confusion about their beliefs. One of the charges was that they practiced cannibalism. It is easy to see how those who did not understand the symbolic language associated with the Last Supper might think this. Another charge was that the Christian religion was really not a religion at all because the followers of it had no images. Another was that they worshipped a man. Early Christian writers had to answer these charges.

Council of Nicaea

After about 200 years of discussion about these issues, a decision was reached in the Council of Nicaea in A.D. 325. Interestingly enough, the long discussion was brought to a head not by the church leaders themselves, but through the interference of the Emperor. The Emperor Constantine had become a Christian. He had a single, unified Empire and wanted but one religion, his own, to prevail in it. He therefore insisted that the various Christian bishops get together and decide the issues about which they were arguing. He decreed that once the vote was taken, it would be binding on everyone. The official position of the church would be what was decided at the Council. The main point which was causing difficulty was the question of the relationship between Christ and God. One party, headed by a man named Arius, insisted that to make Christ equal to God meant that there were really two gods and this could not be, as there was really only one God. Arius said that the Son of God was created by God, sent to earth in the body (incarnate) of Jesus Christ, but that he was not of the same essence or nature as the Father. The opposing position, held by a man named Athanasius, was that the Son of God, incarnate in Christ, was actually of the same nature or substance as the Father. Christ was a human being, but he shared the nature of God. It was the

Flemish minature, 1500 – 1510, from Hours of the Virgin for Roman Use. This picture tells a story. See if you can read it. Here are the symbol meanings: Carnation or pink means "perfect love"; anemone means "sorrow"; orb or globe means "power"; cross means "Christianity." Note that there are twelve beads.
Courtesy of the Pierpont Morgan Library

party of Athanasius which won out at the Council of Nicaea. The results of the Council are summed up in the Creed of the Council of Nicaea. The Nicene Creed which appears at the beginning of this chapter is an expanded version of the Creed of the Council of Nicaea.

As you read this, note that the position of Arius is carefully denied through the precise wording:

The Creed of the Council of Nicaea

We believe in one God the Father All-sovereign, maker of all things visible and invisible;

And in one Lord Jesus Christ, the Son of God, begotten of the Father, only-begotten, that is of the substance of the Father, God of God, Light of Light, true God of true God, begotten not made, of one substance with the Father, through whom all things were made, things in heaven and things on the earth; who for us men and for our salvation came down and was made flesh, and became man, suffered, and rose on the third day, ascended into the heavens, is coming to judge the living and dead.

And in the Holy Spirit.
And those that say 'There was when he was not,'
     and, 'Before he was begotten he was not,'
    and that, 'He came into being from what-is-not,'
or those that allege, that the son of God is
       'Of another substance or essence'
      or 'created,'
      or 'changeable'
      or 'alterable,'
these the Catholic and Apostolic Church anathematizes.[1]

At the council of Nicaea, the doctrine of the Trinity was formulated, although there were points which were clarified and expounded in more detail at succeeding councils. Chief

---

[1] Henry Bettenson, ed. *Documents of the Christian Church* (London: Oxford University Press, 1947), p. 36.

among these was the relationship of the Holy Spirit to the Father and the Son.

The Holy Spirit had always been a part of Jewish thought and played an important role in the New Testament. There were many definitions of it and ideas about it, but they all included the idea of the Holy Spirit as the "inspirer" of prophecy, the agent of revelation and the sustainer of the faithful Christian. What then was its relationship to God? After the Council of Nicaea this question was debated and the conclusion reached that it, too, was of the same substance as the Father. This addition to the findings of the Council of Nicaea is reflected in the longer Nicene Creed. The Roman Church added "and the Son," an addition never accepted by the Eastern Church.

It is interesting to note that the more popular Apostles' Creed leaves out many of the argumentative phrases and presents a more straightforward statement of belief. It was based on an old baptismal formula and was expanded as it was used over the centuries.

The Apostles' Creed

I believe in God the Father Almighty, Maker of heaven and earth: And in Jesus Christ his only Son our Lord: Who was conceived by the Holy Ghost, Born of the Virgin Mary: Suffered under Pontius Pilate, Was crucified, dead and buried: He descended into hell; The third day he rose again from the dead: He ascended into heaven, And sitteth on the right hand of God the Father Almighty: From thence he shall come to judge the quick and the dead.

I believe in the Holy Ghost: The holy Catholic Church; The Communion of Saints: The Forgiveness of sins: The Resurrection of the body: And the life everlasting. Amen.

One of the reasons Athanasius was so insistent upon the person of Christ being in some way that of God himself was that he felt that unless this were true, the whole idea of Christ being able to save man would be impossible. God had to save man. Man was completely incapable of saving himself. A lesser being than God would be helpless in the face of the enormity of the problem. God was the only salvation. If faith in Jesus will save us, then Jesus has to be God. It was as simple as that to Anthanasius. Arius shared these feelings, except that he felt a danger, even a blasphemy, in calling Jesus the same as God because to him this created two Gods which cannot be. Arius favored the idea that God created Christ as a special agent to save men. Would you call Arius' view "liberal," as many have done?

The next problem was to determine how it would be possible for the two natures, divine and human, to exist side by side in the same being. The Council of Nicaea had emphasized, out of necessity, the divine in Jesus. Overemphasizing the divinity of Jesus would lessen the greatness of God. It would limit him in a way which was distasteful to these early Christian thinkers who had inherited from Judaism a thorough-going monotheism with its accompanying lofty conception of God.

The Council of Chalcedon

The Council of Chalcedon which convened in A.D. 451 expressed the new thinking in this way. Note the emphasis on the humanity of Christ.

Therefore, following the holy fathers, we all with one accord teach men to acknowledge one and the same Son, our Lord Jesus Christ, at once complete in Godhead and complete in manhood, truly God and truly man, consisting also of a reasonable soul and body; of one substance with the Father as regards his Godhead, and at the same time of one substance with us as regards his manhood; like us in all respects, apart from sin; as regards his Godhead, begotten of the Father before the ages, but yet as regards his manhood begotten, for us men for our salvation, of Mary the Virgin, the God-bearer; one and the same Christ, Son, Lord, Only-begotten, recognized in two natures, without confusion, without change, without division, without separation; the distinction of natures being in no way annulled by the union, but rather the characteristics of each nature being preserved and coming together to form one person and substance, not as parted or separated into two persons, but one and the same Son and Only-begotten God the Word, Lord Jesus Christ; even as the prophets from earliest times spoke of him, and our Lord Jesus Christ himself taught us, and the creed of the Fathers has handed down to us.[2]

The doctrine of the nature of Christ was now fully thought out. Some never accepted it as the Councils decreed it. With each Council, the defeated party formed a small sect continuing the ideas which it had fought to maintain. Some of these groups are still in existence today in the Near East. Why was it so many people did accept the doctrine?

Christ as Intermediary

A problem arises in every religion at the point when God is recognized as being all-powerful, almighty, the ruler of the whole universe. This places God a long way from poor, weak man. Such a concept of God is almost impossible to imagine, and it becomes unbelievable that a God like this would be interested in such a mite as man. It becomes even more incomprehensible that God would care for the individual. Therefore, a search begins for some way in which to reach

[2] Bettenson, *op. cit.*, pp. 72-73.

God, and often the solution is found in an intermediary, some being who can act as a sort of messenger between man and God. In this way, man can reach God and work toward achieving his salvation with some assurance that his prayers and his efforts will be effective to this end. In Christianity, Christ became the intermediary. Since he was fully human, he was close to lowly man. The worshipper could relate to him, could feel that Christ had lived as had the worshipper himself, and had suffered, and so was closer to him than God could ever be. Christ was human, but also divine. There could be only one God. Worshipping Christ was, therefore, worshipping God, not a man.

The development of the Last Supper into the sacrament of the Mass is also a part of the Christian quest for a closer relationship to the God of the universe. The communal meal, celebrated in the early church became a token meal with only the bread and the wine to symbolize the Last Supper. The bread represented the body of Christ and the wine his blood. To meet the interpretation given by the people that in some mysterious way the bread and the wine actually changed into the body and blood of Christ, a theory was worked out which held that only the essence changed. The bread still remained bread and the wine remained wine to all outward appearances. This theory is called transubstantiation. The worshipper, by partaking of the elements, as they are called, actually eats the body and drinks the blood of Christ. By so doing he partakes of the divine and so comes closer to God. This theory is based on the same idea as that of Christ and God being the same, yet different.

The Middle Ages

During the Middle Ages, the church's teaching was accepted concerning all of these things. People did not reason

Jesus dressed in fifteenth century style, fifteenth century Flemish
miniature from Hours of the Virgin
Courtesy of the Pierpont Morgan Library

them out, but assumed they were true. Imagine, if you will, living in an age when only a few people could read and write. Even those who possessed knowledge had a limited chance to exercise it because books were scarce since they were all copied by hand. Libraries, bookshops, even schools as we know them were nonexistent. How would you obtain your knowledge? How would you know whether what you believed was true? How could you check?

It was essential for the church to devise ways by which believers could learn of the Christian teaching and remember it, and to this necessity we owe much of our great art. In addition to teaching and preaching, statues depicted the main characters in the drama of the life of Jesus, the stations of the cross helped people remember the events in his life. Love of God through Christ was depicted in beautiful stained glass windows and in elaborate altars. The mystery of the presence of God himself on each and every altar was celebrated in elaborate altar cloths and in beautiful carvings. Paintings of Jesus done during this period often show him in a contemporary setting. People felt he was one of them. By showing him in familiar surroundings and dress, they felt somehow closer to God and they found it easier to understand the events of his life if they were in "modern dress."

The divine in Christ was emphasized by the regard with which the elements of the Mass were treated. Sometime during the period, the wine was no longer given to the communicants because it was so easily spilled, and since it was the blood of Christ, this was a serious thing indeed. The crumbs of the bread were also carefully guarded. And so, on the other hand, the Middle Ages made Jesus closer to the ordinary man by picturing him as one of us; on the other, his divinity was emphasized by the miracle of the Mass.

The Reformation

The Reformation of the sixteenth century, from which stemmed the Protestant churches, changed the emphasis of the earlier Roman Catholic Church upon the elaboration of the events in the life of Jesus to a much more austere view of him. This change in emphasis was caused by a number of factors, but among them all one invention stands out as the most influential. Imagine what would happen in an age when few could read and write if an invention were made which would enable those who could read to obtain more books. What would be the result? Would this affect belief? Such an invention was that of the printing press around the year 1450. A whole new world opened up. No longer would people have to rely on hearsay and memory. They could read to obtain knowledge. With more books available, more people learned to read. The first books to be printed with this new invention were Bibles. There are still in existence "Gutenberg Bibles" named after the man who printed them. What do you think happened to the legends and myths which had sprung up over the centuries about Jesus? What of the teachings of the Church which seemed to run counter to the New Testament itself?

The great reformers such as Martin Luther and John Calvin, coming as they did after the invention of printing, insisted on a return to Scripture. This they could do because now Bibles were more readily available. They scanned the pages of the New Testament where they sought to find out the truth about the life of Jesus. Since they pushed aside all that was not actually found in the New Testament, their life of Jesus was not nearly as colorful as those of the Middle Ages. In trying to understand Jesus, they relied heavily on Paul and his interpretation of Jesus to help with the difficult questions of the nature of Christ. They also accepted the findings of the early Church Councils, Nicaea and Chalcedon, which had further explained the nature of the Savior and solved problems raised, but not answered, in the New Testament. However, the ultimate authority for Protestants became the Bible, not the church. This has led, of course, to many opinions regarding the interpretation of the Bible, because each person who reads it may interpret it differently. And so, there have arisen many denominations with different beliefs and divergent practices based on differences in Biblical interpretation.

One example of this is the Last Supper. The reformers read about it in the New Testament and interpreted what they read there to mean that Jesus instructed that everyone should have both the bread and the wine, rather than just the bread as in Catholic practice. They disagreed among themselves concerning the exact nature of the elements, but all agreed that they did not actually turn into the body and blood of Christ as Catholics believed. The result was that there is down to this day a wide variety of practices within Protestantism in celebrating Communion, and different interpretations of the exact nature of this sacrament as well.

There are among the denominations some, in the liberal group, who go a step further than the Reformation leaders and reject the ancient theory that man is evil and totally helpless. Not only can he interpret Scripture for himself, they hold, but he can aid in his own salvation. Not only can he use his reason, he is obliged to use it in developing his religious philosophy. There are many who add to this faith in man an emphasis on this life, saying that life on earth is lived but once, so that our concern should be not with the other world and what will happen to us after death, but with this world. To such, man's duty is to make it the best possible world in which to live. They hold that this is what God demands of men, not particular beliefs.

And so we return to the quotation which is found at the beginning of this book:

And Jesus went on with his disciples to the villages of Caesarea Philippi; and on the way he asked his disciples. "Who do men say that I am?" And they told him, "John the Baptist; and others say, Elijah; and others one of the prophets." And he asked them, "But who do you say that I am?"

Mark 8:27-29
Revised Standard Version

Bibliography

General Reference Books

The following books are selected as the most up-to-date and useful references to go with this study. A library should consider having all of them available. Individuals interested in Biblical study will find them a constant source of information. If only one is to be purchased, it is suggested that it be the Peake Commentary.

Peake's Commentary on the Bible, ed. Black, Matthew and Rowley, H. H., Thomas Nelson and Sons, 1962. $15.00.
In one volume, background material and interpretation of individual passages. Maps in the back.

Hastings Dictionary of the Bible (revised edition), Charles Scribner's Sons, 1963. $15.00.
A short encyclopedia containing articles on almost everything of interest to the student of the Bible.

Our Living Bible, by Avi-Yonah, M. and Kraeling, E. McGraw-Hill, 1962. $15.00.
Profusely illustrated, this volume considers each book in the Bible in turn, giving the results of archaeological discoveries to fill in the background. Not a commentary, but a useful and beautiful supplement to one.

Special Reference Books

Nelson's Complete Concordance of the Revised Standard Version Bible. Thomas Nelson and Sons, 1957. $15.00.

Nelson's Concise Concordance of the Revised Standard Version Bible. Thomas Nelson and Sons, 1959. $2.50.
The first is complete, the second is selective. One or the other should certainly be on hand.

Gospel Parallels, Throckmorton, Burton H., Jr., editor. Thomas Nelson and Sons, 1957, $3.00.
Should be on hand for consultation and convenience in comparing passages.

Picture References

Since only a limited number of pictures could be included in this book, it is urged that others be sought to give visual reality to the wide variation in interpretation of Jesus and the events of his life.

There are many beautiful and usually expensive books containing reproductions of paintings. These can sometimes be obtained from a library, and will add much to the enjoyment of the study.

The following books are paperbacks. Since they are not expensive, the pictures in them could be cut out and mounted so that an individual collection of illustrations could be made. They have been listed by publisher.

World of Art Paperbacks. Frederick A. Praeger, 64 University Place, New York, N.Y.
RICE, DAVID T. *Art of the Byzantine Era.*
MURRAY, PETER. *Art of the Renaissance.*

Compass History of Art Series. The Viking Press, 625 Madison Ave. New York. N.Y.
Most useful volumes are:
Early Christian Painting.
Christian and Byzantine Painting.
Romanesque Painting.
Gothic Painting.
Renaissance Painting.

Mentor-UNESCO Art Books. The New American Library, 501 Madison Avenue, New York, N.Y.
This series includes three volumes which would be useful. There are not as many pictures in these as in the ones listed above, but they are equally beautiful.
Byzantine Frescoes.
Spanish Frescoes.
Russian Icons.

All of the series listed above have some, or all, of the pictures in color. There are some others which have only black and white, but which are of great value because they are selected for specific subjects.
Harper Men of Wisdom Series, Harper and Row, 49 East 33rd St., New York, N.Y.
STEINMANN, JEAN *Saint John the Baptist and the Desert Tradition.*
TRESMONTANT, CLAUDE *Saint Paul and the Mystery of Christ.*

Bantam Gallery Edition. Bantam Books, 271 Madison Ave., New York, N.Y.
CHAMBERLAYNE, ELIZABETH. *The Life of Christ.*

Other Helpful and Interesting Books

BAINTON, ROLAND. *Early Christianity.* Anvil Original, 1960.
A good, short history of the earliest centuries of Christianity. Part two contains documents and readings to go along with it.

GASTER, THEODOR H. *The Dead Sea Scriptures.* Doubleday Anchor Paperback.
A translation of the Dead Sea Scrolls with an introduction telling about them.

BETTENSON, HENRY. *Documents of the Christian Church.* Oxford University Press, 1947.
A useful and fascinating collection of primary sources, including the creeds and various readings from the leaders of the Reformation.

BARRETT, C. K. *The New Testament Background: Selected Documents.* Harper Torchbooks, 1961.
The title is descriptive. The book contains readings from Roman histories, philosophers, Maccabees, Josephus, apocalyptic writers and others.

GOODSPEED, EDGAR J. *Paul.* Apex Books.
A good, readable biography of Paul by the famous New Testament scholar.

Written for Young People, but Adults Will Benefit!

BAINTON, ROLAND. *The Church of Our Fathers.* Charles Scribner's Sons, 1950.
A history of the Christian Church from its beginnings to the present, told in lively fashion and charmingly illustrated. A must!

BOUQUET, A. C. *Everyday Life in New Testament Times.* Charles Scribner's Sons, 1953.
Good reference for looking up all sorts of facts not easy to find elsewhere. Informative on the subject of its title.

FOSDICK, HARRY EMERSON. *The Life of Saint Paul.* Random House, a Landmark Book, 1962.
Brief biography of Paul by the famous New York clergyman.

HONOUR, ALAN. *Cave of Riches.* McGraw-Hill, Whittlesey House, 1956.
Exciting book written in novel form based on the discovery of the Dead Sea Scrolls.